Best Restaurants® San & Francisco & Northern California

By the Editors of
California Critic

Jacqueline Killeen
Charles C. Miller
Sharon Silva

Illustrations: Roy Killeen
Design: Lynne Parode

101 Productions
San Francisco

TO THE CALIFORNIA CRITIC SUBSCRIBERS
in grateful acknowledgement of their assistance
in evaluating the restaurants herein.

Published by 101 Productions, Inc.
834 Mission Street, San Francisco, California 94103
Distributed to the book trade in the United States
by Charles Scribner's Sons, New York

Library of Congress Cataloging in Publication Data

Killeen, Jacqueline.
    Best restaurants, San Francisco & Northern California.

    1. Restaurants, lunchrooms, etc.–California–
Directories.   2. San Francisco–Restaurants–
Directories.   I. Miller, Charles C., joint author.
II. Silva, Sharon, joint author.   3. Title.
TX907.K483   1977   647'.95794   77-8516

ISBN 0-89286-117-7

Contents

Introduction

THIS BOOK does not pretend to be an all-inclusive encyclopedia of Northern California restaurants. Instead we have selected only the best restaurants in all price ranges, representing a variety of ethnic cuisines.

You may well ask how we know they are the best and what is our criteria of "the best." Our selections are based, first, on a decade of professional experience in evaluating restaurants. This guide was first published in 1968 with the title *101 Nights in California* and has been revised seven times subsequently. During these years our team of reviewers, all lifelong Californians, have dined at thousands of restaurants in order to cull out the best.

But even more significantly, these choices have been affirmed for this edition by thousands of discriminating Californians who dine out constantly. No other guide can make this claim. We were able to obtain this unique feedback only because we publish a private newsletter on restaurants and wines, *California Critic.* Before revising this current edition of the book, we compiled a list of the restaurants we were considering for the guide and sent it to our newsletter subscribers, asking them to evaluate, on a 1 to 10 scale, those restaurants in which they had dined recently. Their opinions were weighed carefully in making our final selections. Thus we can truthfully say that our selections were based, not on one or two recent visits to a restaurant, but in some cases on as many as 100 visits within the past year.

Our criteria? The food—its quality and imagination—is our primary consideration. No matter how magnificent a restaurant's decor, no matter how proficient the service, no matter how formidable its reputation, we do not include a restaurant if we have not found the food to be consistently first-rate. We are also very old-fashioned in our notions about what constitutes first-rate cooking. Vegetables must be fresh, likewise the seafood if so advertised. Soups, sauces and the like must be prepared from scratch. Ditto for desserts, even though these might come from a nearby bakery rather than the restaurant's own kitchen. In short, if we find any evidence of extensive use of canned or frozen foods, of convenience foods, or of misrepresentation of items on the menu, we will not recommend a restaurant for this book.

To help you find a restaurant to match your budget for the evening, we have divided our selections into categories of inexpensive, moderate and expensive, using the symbols shown below. We have based the ratings on the price of an average three-course dinner in that restaurant, food only; cocktails, wine and tips would be extra. In many restaurants, you could end up spending more if you splurged or less if you tightened your belt. Prices quoted in this book were in effect at the time of publication and are subject to change at any time.

$ **UNDER $6** The food will be good as well as economical, but atmosphere and smooth service may be lacking at some of these restaurants. Dress is most always casual.

$$ **UNDER $12** In this price range of $6 to $12, we expect some charm and atmosphere in addition to excellent food. Many, but not all, of these restaurants are informal and the service might not always be highly professional.

$$$ **OVER $12** At this price, we demand perfection in every department. The food must be exceptional, the service flawless and the surroundings magnificent.

It should go without saying that our visits to restaurants are anonymous, that we always pay our own restaurant check, that there is no charge to a restaurant to appear in this book. In fact there is absolutely no way a restaurant could buy or bribe its way into any of our publications.

A GUIDE FOR LOVERS OF FRESH FISH

Fresh seafood is not as readily available in Northern California restaurants as one might expect in a coastal area. And all restaurants are not as honest as they should be in stating what is fresh and what is frozen. It is helpful to know which fish are readily available fresh and the seasons when they are plentiful. Following are some guidelines, compiled with the cooperation of some of the leading suppliers of seafood to restaurants.

FRESH WEST COAST FISH
AVAILABLE YEAR-ROUND

A variety of white fish from California waters is available fresh all year, except when bad weather keeps the fishing boats ashore. These include the small, delicate rex sole and sand dabs, red snapper and a number of larger fish served as "filet of sole"—petrale, Pacific "Dover" and "English" sole (which are inferior to their European namesakes) and flounder. True sea bass comes in fresh from Southern California; ling cod and cod come fresh from northern waters and are sometimes sold as sea bass filets. Fresh rock cod is sometimes sold as snapper. Rainbow trout is brought in fresh from Idaho throughout the year, but in the average restaurant it is more likely to be frozen. Squid is usually fresh.

SEASONAL WEST COAST FISH

The season for California's silver salmon extends from April through the summer, although fresh salmon from other areas is sometimes found in the better restaurants outside of these dates. Northern halibut appears fresh most commonly in May and June, although it is obtainable through the summer. A few restaurants get fresh swordfish from southern California, but usually it is frozen.

WEST COAST SHELLFISH

California's Dungeness crab is available fresh from November through June, but is at its peak in both quantity and quality early in the season. Alaskan king crab is served at other times of the year and is most often frozen. California baby shrimp in their shells can be obtained fresh from mid-April to September, but most restaurants buy them frozen, picked and cleaned. Oysters are brought in fresh from Tomales and Inverness or from Puget Sound in all but the summer months. California lobster, sometimes called crayfish, are considerably smaller than their Eastern cousins and are available from October 1 to March 15.

EAST COAST SEAFOOD

Many better restaurants in Northern California feature seafood which is flown in fresh from the East Coast. Cherrystone and littleneck clams, blue point oysters and Maine lobster are readily available throughout the year. Fresh mussels appear on menus from late fall to spring. Eastern scallops and Maryland soft shell crabs are occasionally found fresh, but in most restaurants they are frozen.

FROZEN SEAFOOD

California restaurants are renowned for abalone, but ironically abalone is always frozen, by law, and most of it comes from Mexico. Even so it can be magnificent when prepared with skill, but tough and dreadful when not cooked properly. Be wary also of low-priced abalone; the better grades are always expensive. Prawns and shrimp (except for the local baby shrimp) are never found fresh in California. Lobster tail, frogs legs and pompano are also always frozen. Many of the seafoods which are available fresh are sold in frozen form out of season. And, of course, many restaurants never serve fresh seafood at all.

A PRIMER OF CALIFORNIA WINES

Northern California is one of the world's great wine-producing areas. Yet many of our most exciting wines—those
from the small or family-owned vineyards—seldom find
their way out of the state. Until recently, the labels of these
vintners rarely appeared on a restaurant wine list. Today,
however, the more conscientious restaurateurs are making
an effort to seek out and to stock the state's lesser-known
wines. Sampling these by ordering blindly a bottle from a
winery you have never before encountered, can be one of
the high adventures in dining out in California.

Unlike the mass-produced, quality-controlled wines of
the industry giants, these esoteric bottlings are very personal statements of the winemaker's taste. Some will be
frankly experimental, and in any case the same varietal
from the same winery will generally vary from year to year.
At the end of this section we have listed the small wineries
which we feel are doing an exceptional job. This is not to
say that we always like all of their wines, but indicates that
tasting them will usually be an experience we are not likely
to forget.

THE PREMIUM VARIETALS
A California premium wine is named not for the district
in which the grape is grown, as in Europe, but for the
principal grape variety it contains. State law prohibits a
winery from calling a wine by this varietal name unless it
contains at least 51 percent of its namesake grape in the
case of a non-vintage wine, and at least 75 percent of that
grape when the wine is vintage dated. Some wines are 100
percent pure varietal, but most are blended to a degree with

other grapes, not purely for expediency, but often to improve the character and taste of the wine. California premium wines are all made from *vinifera* grapes of European origin, whereas many wines produced in the Eastern United States are made from the *labrusca* grape, native to North America. Following is a description of the major varietal wines produced in California, with their European counterparts.

WHITE WINES

Chardonnay, the principal grape used in the white wines of Chablis, Macon and other areas of Burgundy, is the giant of the California whites. Chardonnays are usually crisp, dry wines of considerable body, often oak-flavored from the casks in which they are aged. Chardonnay mellows with some age; it's at its best after three years in the bottle.

Pinot Blanc, another white grape of Burgundy, produces a light, dry wine, which is best drunk young.

Sauvignon Blanc is a principal grape in the white Bordeaux wines of Sauternes and Graves; its wines range from semisweet to dry. Some vintners market Sauvignon Blanc as **Fumé Blanc**, which is made to resemble a dry, oaky wine of the Loire Valley. **Semillon** is another principal component of Sauternes. It is a fruity wine which ranges from sweet to dry, with the best dry Semillons coming from California's Livermore Valley.

Chenin Blanc is responsible for the Vouvray wine of the Loire Valley and thus is sometimes labeled **Pineau de la Loire.** Traditionally a fragrant wine with a hint of sweetness, Chenin Blanc is now being produced by some wineries in ultra-dry versions which still retain the flavor and delicacy of the grape.

Johannisberg Riesling is named for the vineyard which produces the noblest of Germany's Rhine wines. Its Californian relatives are fruity, flowery and range from dry to slightly sweet.

Sylvaner Riesling is another German grape, most abundantly grown in the less distinguished wine-producing areas of Germany. It produces a pale, light wine which does not aspire to the greatness of its Johannisberg cousin.

Gewurztraminer is native to Alsace and in California produces a zesty, fruity wine of medium dryness which can hold its own as an accompaniment to hot and spicy foods.

ROSE WINES

Traditionally the pink wines called rosé are made from the sweet, rather insipid **Grenache** grape from the Rhone Val-

ley. Lately a number of California vintners have started making rosé varietals with much more character from the **Zinfandel, Gamay** and **Cabernet** grapes.

RED WINES

Cabernet Sauvignon, the mighty grape which produces the great clarets of Bordeaux, is king of the California reds. The best Cabernets are big complex wines of outstanding bouquet that improve dramatically with age. They are drinkable at age four or five, remarkable twice that old, and can be extraordinary when aged 15 to 20 years.

Merlot is a principal grape in Bordeaux' St. Emilion district. It was brought to California primarily for blending with Cabernet. Some California vintners have just recently started bottling this straight as a soft, dry varietal.

Pinot Noir produces the robust, full-bodied red wines of Burgundy, although most of their California cousins tend to be lighter. Pinot Noir usually reaches its peak after three to five years in the bottle.

Gamay and Gamay Beaujolais grapes come from the Beaujolais area of Burgundy. In California they produce fruity wines, light in body and color, which are best in their youth.

Petite Sirah, a grape of the Rhone Valley, produces a mellow, dry wine which improves noticeably with age and serves well as a companion to hearty foods.

Zinfandel is California's most interesting grape. Though a *vinifera* variety, the mystery of its European origins has never been solved. Zinfandels vary enormously depending upon where and how they are produced. Some are light and zesty, lovely when young; others when aged achieve a body, complexity and bouquet comparable to a great Cabernet.

Barbera, a native of Piedmonte, was brought to California by Italian immigrants. It produces a hearty, full-bodied wine best suited to Italian foods. Lighter Italian varietals, not so often encountered, are **Grignolino** and **Charbono**.

GENERIC WINES

When you buy wines simply labeled Chablis, Sauterne, Burgundy, Rosé, Riesling or suchlike—with no varietal designation—you are casting yourself on the mercy of the winemaker. You can be sure only that the wine is either white or red or pink, for there are no restrictions whatsoever on what goes into the blend. (A generic "Riesling" for example, need not even be made from grapes of German origin.) With a few notable exceptions, you can be reasonably sure that these blends contain the vintners' most inferior and inexpensive grapes. Most of the "house wines" sold by the glass or by the carafe in restaurants are generic wines, produced and bottled in bulk, and sold at a markup that is often double the profit the restaurant would realize from the sale of a premium varietal. Generally by spending very little more you can enjoy a premium wine.

CALIFORNIA'S SMALL WINERIES

Following is a list of some small California wineries producing wines of premium quality. Their bottlings are highly individualistic, usually intriguing. One of these labels on a wine list is an invitation to adventurous wine tasting.

David Bruce	Chateau Montelena
Burgess Cellars	Montevina
Chalone Vineyard	Mount Eden
Clos du Val	Oakville
Cuvaison	Parducci
Dry Creek	Joseph Phelps
Fetzer Vineyards	Ridge Vineyards
Freemark Abbey	Schramsberg
Gemello	Spring Mountain
Hacienda	Stag's Leap
Hanzell Vineyards	Sterling
Heitz Wine Cellars	Stonegate
Husch	Sutter Home
Llords & Elwood	Joseph Swan
Mayacamas	Veedercrest Vineyards

San Francisco

R. KILLEEN.

San Francisco: Nob Hill
ALEXIS
Russian/French

$$$

Alexis has retired, but maître d' André and Alexis' long-time chefs carry on the grand traditions of this opulent restaurant. You dine here in czarist splendor, watched over by four life-size mosaic icons. Service and atmosphere are vastly better in the large front room where the VIPs are seated; ask for a table there when you reserve. Dinners are all à la carte and a selection from the hors d'oeuvre is a must. For the big splurge try the blini with caviar and sour cream. We also highly recommend the dolma, pâté maison in a puff pastry crust, crab crêpes Bengal or the langoustines Alexis. The cold, clarified borscht passé is outstanding. Entrée prices are à la carte. The lamb dishes are among the house specialties, as is the Dover sole, flown fresh from England. We have not had much luck with desserts, here; invest in the hors d'oeuvre instead. The European wine list is expensive; California selections are limited and highly priced. After dinner, be sure to visit the romantic cellar for a drink and gypsy music.

ALEXIS, 1001 California Street, San Francisco. Telephone: (415) 885-6400. Hours: 5-midnight; closed Sunday. Cards: AE, CB, DC, MC. Reservations advised. Valet parking. Full bar service. Coat and tie required.

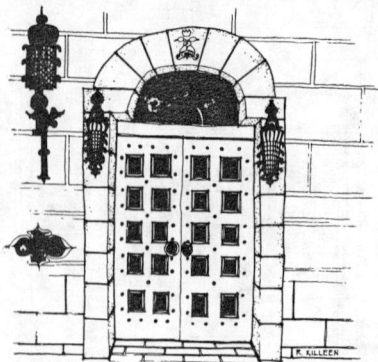

Les Hors d'Oeuvres

Blini à la Russe, with Caviar and Sour Cream 13.50

Beluga Caviar, Malasol (per ounce) 17.50	Paté Maison 2.50
Blue Point Oysters on Half Shell . 3.75	Foie Gras de Strasbourg 8.00
Olympia Oyster Cocktail 3.50	Yalanji Dolma 2.75
Shrimp Cocktail 3.50	Melon or Papaya with Parma Ham 3.50
Marinated Bismark Herring . . . 3.00	Stuffed Avocado Alexis 3.75
Nova Scotia Smoked Salmon . . 4.50	Escargots de Bourgogne 3.75
Quenelles Nantua 3.50	Shrimps Joinville 3.75
Crab Crepes Bengal 3.50	Langoustines Alexis 4.75

Grillades

Brochette of Beef Tenderloin . . 10.00	Rack of Lamb, Karski 13.75
French Cut Lamb Chops 11.50	Filet of Lamb, Alexis (for Two) . . 28.50
Minute Steak 9.75	Filet Mignon 10.75
Broiled Dover Sole 10.75	New York Cut Sirloin 10.75
Half Broiled Chicken 6.75	Châteaubriand Forestiere (for Two) 23.00

Poissons

Dover Sole Meuniere 10.75	Louisiana Frog Legs Provençale . 8.50
Dover Sole, Waleska 11.25	Poached Salmon, Alexis 9.00
Coquille St. Jacques Saute . . . 7.50	Lobster Cardinal 12.75
Filet of Rex Sole, Meuniere . . . 7.25	Crab Legs, Véronique 8.75

Entrees

Chicken à la Kiev	7.75
Boneless Squab, Byzantine	9.25
Chicken Casserole Grand Mere	14.50
Pheasant, Souvoroff (For Two)	28.00
Pheasant, Smetana (For Two)	26.00
Canard à l'Orange (For Two)	18.50
Grenadins of Veal, Alexis	10.75
Beef Strogonoff	9.75
Médaillon de Boeuf, Alexis	10.50
Steak au Poivre	10.75
Steak Tartare	10.25
Steak Diane	10.75
Tournedos Rossini	11.75

Koulebiaka à la Russe, Salmon or Chicken, (24 Hours Notice Required) for Two 24.00

San Francisco: North Beach
BEETHOVEN
German

$$

An Old World aura pervades the dimly lit dining room with its dark wood wainscoting, large oil paintings, red-flowered curtains and matching wall covering. Even the sounds are European, from the classical taped music to the continental accents of much of the clientele. If you think of German food as being too heavy, you'll be pleasantly surprised by the light touch imparted by the Swiss-born owners. Dinners include a freshly made soup, often a superb cream of vegetable, and a salad of butter lettuce and mushrooms with a tart mustard dressing. Beethoven's sauerbraten is one of the best local versions; the beef is tender, marinated two weeks, and the beautifully flavored sauce is enhanced with plumped raisins. Another favorite is the schweinebraten, slices of roast pork sauced with pan juices. The veal here is tender, though not white, and cooked with a rich marsala sauce and mushrooms. Entrées are accompanied either with crisp potato pancakes or spätzle, and red cabbage or fresh vegetables. The desserts here have been a disappointment, but who needs them. A complimentary glass of port ends the meal.

BEETHOVEN RESTAURANT, 1701 Powell Street, San Francisco. Telephone: (415) 391-4488. Hours: 5:30-10, Monday-Saturday. Cards: BA, MC. Reservations advised. Beer and wine only. Street parking.

Dinners

includes . Soup of the day . Tossed green Salad
Vegetable and Garnie
Coffee

Hungarian Galasch with Spätzle	$ 5.65
Schweinebraten	5.75
Roast Pork with Potatoe Pancakes and Red Cabbage	
Chicken	5.25
in Wine sauce and Mushrooms	
Trout	5.35
sauted with Lemon Butter, Capers	
Shellfish Saute "Provençale"	6.50
Stuffed Cabbage "hausfrauenart"	4.75
Sauerbraten	5.85
Beef marinated in Red Wine and Herbs served with Red Cabbage and Potatoe Pancakes	
Rindsrouladen	5.85
Stuffed Rolled Beef in Burgundy Sauce with Red Cabbage and Potatoe Pancakes	
Wienerschnitzel	6.75
Breaded Veal cutlet with Parsley Potatoes	
Geschnezeltes Kalbfleisch "Marsala"	6.45
Sliced Veal in Marsala sauce and Mushrooms	
Zwiebelroastbraten	6.95
N.Y. Sirlion Steak with sauted Onions	
N.Y. Sirlion Steak Prime Choice	7.25
Duckling in Orange Sauce	6.95

San Francisco: Financial District
BLUE FOX
Italian/Continental

$$$

Today one of San Francisco's most opulent and highly respected restaurants, the Blue Fox has a history as colorful and often unrespectable as the city itself. It sprung from the ashes of 1906 as a one-room cafe across from the City Jail, became a popular hangout for lawyers and judges, and was a notorious speakeasy of the 1920s. When Mario Mondin acquired it in 1942, the Blue Fox was still a humble and crowded single room serving "deluxe" dinners for under $2. Today the jail has moved across town and $2 will not even buy an hors d'oeuvre. Over the years the Blue Fox has expanded into three gracious dining rooms, lavishly appointed with high-backed velvet chairs, mirrors, gold and crystal chandeliers, mostly imported from Europe. The Blue Fox is à la carte, expensive and worth it! A selection from the 27 appetizers is difficult. We have found the pasta—tortellini or fettuccine—outstanding. And, of the soups, the cream of spinach is superb. Veal dishes are among the house specialties and although the veal is not milk fed, it is thin and tender. The squab stuffed with wild rice is a great favorite and all the beef is USDA prime. Fresh vegetables, cooked with imagination and respect, accompany the entrées. For early diners (before 7:30), the Blue Fox serves a five-course dinner at a fixed price of $12.50. And for private parties of 12 or more, there are two ornately decorated wine-cellar rooms.

BLUE FOX RESTAURANT, 659 Merchant Street, San Francisco. Telephone: (415) 981-1177. Hours: 6-11, Monday-Saturday. Cards: AE, BA, CB, DC, MC. Reservations advised. Full bar service. Valet parking.

A La Carte

Entreés

Breast of Chicken Escoffier	7.50
Breast of Chicken Jerusalem	7.75
Boneless Squab Montmorency, Wild Rice	10.50
Long Island Duckling Flambé aux Cerises Noir (for two)	18.00
Filets de Rex Sole Meunière	7.50
Filets de Sole Veronique	8.00
Poached Fresh Salmon, Hollandaise	8.75
Frog Legs Sautes Provencal	8.50
Gamberi della Casa con Risotto	9.00
Lobster Tail en Chemise	13.50
Veal Sweetbreads Sauté au Sherry	8.00
Veal Sweetbreads Venitienne	8.25
Veal Scaloppine Marsala	8.50
Saltimbocca della Casa	8.75
Piccata di Vitello con Carciofini	8.75
Escalopes de Veau Lorraine	9.00
Noisettes of Lamb Antoinette	12.50
Rack of Lamb Garni (for two)	25.00
Chateau de Boeuf Strasbourg en Chemise (for two)	28.00

Grillades

Brochette of Tenderloin with Wild Rice	8.00
Médaillon de Boeuf aux Champignons	9.00
New York Cut (Sirloin of Beef)	10.50
Double French Lamb Chops	11.00
Tournedos à la Gastronome	12.00

San Francisco: Mission District
AUX DELICES
Vietnamese

$

This is one of the newest of the rash of Vietnamese restaurants to open recently in San Francisco and it is decidedly one of the best. As you enter the dimly lit little dining room, the near-overwhelming fragrance of exotic spices gives the first clue to the good things to come. Aux Delices offers some 55 Vietnamese dishes nightly, a quartette of French specialties and, incongruously, a selection of East Coast submarine sandwiches, served at lunch. Dinners ($2.60 to $5) come with a thick, lemony chicken-rice soup, but do try some of the à la carte appetizers as well. We particularly recommend bo chanh, a tart salad of shredded lettuce, cucumbers and beef, flavored with lemon and spices; or banh cuon, savory bits of meats and vegetables steamed in a rice paste, somewhat like the Chinese dim sum. One favorite among the entrées is the stuffed sweet and sour chicken: A thin shell of boned breast encases a rich forcemeat, all topped with a colorful sauce containing chunks of pineapple and sliced carrots. The most unusual dish, however, is tom chien, a spectacular platter of large shrimp, assorted cold vegetable slices and dipping sauces. With this come paper-thin pancakes made of shrimp dough, in which you wrap the shrimp and vegetables—sort of a Vietnamese taco! There is also a selection of stir-fry dishes and mild curries, many of which are served on a sizzling hot metal plate set in a wooden platter—so hot that clouds of white steam rise in the air.

AUX DELICES, 1002 Potrero Avenue, San Francisco. Telephone: (415) 285-3196. Lunch: 11-3, Monday-Saturday. Dinner: 5-10, nightly. No cards. Reservations advised. Beer and wine only.

San Francisco: Downtown
CAFE MOZART
Continental

$

This tiny coffee house is as European as the name suggests. There are only five marble-topped tables and a counter filled with luscious pastries in two sunny, high-ceilinged rooms. An enormous gilt-edged antique mirror on one wall makes the space seem larger. Strains of Mozart and other classical composers fill the air. Cafe Mozart serves a fine selection of specialty coffees and teas, plus an assortment of pastries and light repasts, priced from $1.50 to $4.25. The egg dishes are elegant, such as eggs Rossini—two beautifully poached eggs served with goose liver pâté, Madeira sauce and truffles. The salad Nicoise, made with white albacore tuna, is first-rate, as is a delicate bouchée à la reine—a pastry shell containing veal, chicken and mushrooms in a light white wine sauce. Pâté with Cumberland sauce, marinated salmon and Welsh rarebit complete the menu. Cafe Mozart is only a few doors up Bush Street from the Powell Street cable car, two blocks down from the top of Nob Hill and two blocks up from Union Square.

CAFE MOZART, 708 Bush Street, San Francisco. Telephone: (415) 391-8480. Hours: 10-3; closed Tuesday. No cards. Reservations accepted. Wine only.

San Francisco: North Beach
CAFFE SPORT
Italian (Sicilian)

$$

Chef/artist Tony La Tona has created a floor-to-ceiling assemblage of memorabilia in his small cafe. There's scarcely an inch of wall or table space that is not ornately carved or covered with collages of old posters or assemblages of seashells, statuary, cookware. Bottles, lanterns, Italian coppa and cheeses hang from the beams. Tony's artistry is also evident in the Sicilian seafood and pastas that come from the kitchen. There is a magnificent whole lobster (sufficient for two) bathed with lemon, garlic and wine, served with a platter of pasta. Calamari is great here also, sometimes fried, sometimes covered in a rich tomato sauce. Scampi are served on a huge platter with mushrooms and a wine-garlic-caper sauce. The pasta is always the tubular, ridged rigatoni, sauced in various ways: smothered with baby shrimp and freshly grated Parmesan; perfumed by basil in a pesto version; covered with a combination of seafoods. Reservations are not accepted and Tony's clientele is usually lined up to fill the first dinner seating at 6:30. If you don't get a seat then, it will be 8 o'clock before the first tables start clearing. Dinners with a green salad range from $5 to $9. During the day Caffe Sport serves gigantic Italian sandwiches of coppa, salami, mortadella on slabs of French bread.

CAFFE SPORT & TRATTORIA, 574 Green Street, San Francisco. Telephone: (415) 981-1251. Hours: 11 am-11 pm, Tuesday-Saturday; dinners start at 6:30. No cards. Reservations not accepted. Full bar service. Inexpensive parking at Vallejo and Powell garage.

CAFFÈ SPORT MENU

PASTA AL FORNO	6.50
PASTA CON SARDE	5.00
PASTA PIZZAIOLA	7.50
PASTA CON MELANZANE	5.00
PASTA CON CARNE E FUNGHI	5.00
PASTA RUSTICA ALLA CARRETTIERA	5.50
PASTA CON PESTO	5.00
PASTA CON VONGOLE	5.50
CALAMARI SAUTE	6.00
CALAMARI IN INSALATA	5.50
CALAMARI FRITTI	7.00
ARAGOSTA (LOBSTER)	9.50
SCAMPI (PRAWNS) ALL' ANTONIO	8.75
SALMONE ALLA PIRATA	7.00
COMBINATION PLATE (CALAMARI, PRAWNS, CLAMS)	8.50
FRIED COMBINATION (CALAMARI, PRAWNS, SCALOPS)	9.25
MELANZANE ALLA PALERMITANA	5.50
PETRALE SOLE	7.00
STEAMED CLAMS	7.50
SPECIAL GREEN SALAD	3.50
GAMBERI IN INSALATA	9.25
CRAB MEAT SALAD	11.75
ARAGOSTA IN INSALATA	10.50
*PIZZA ALLA PALERMITANA	

(24 HR. NOTICE & SERVES AFTER 11:30)

*SPECIAL MONDAY & SATURDAY ONLY (ASK WAITER)

San Francisco:
Marina and Downtown
CARAVANSARY
Mediterranean

$$

Setrak Injaian, whose father was a chef to Middle Eastern royalty, started serving quiches in his Chestnut Street gourmet shop a few years ago and soon he had a full-fledged restaurant in the back of the store. A second restaurant above his new Sutter Street shop is now the most interesting place to eat in the downtown shopping area. The dining room here is quite spacious, walls lined with cookware, tables covered with gold cloths, sun-splashed on clear days. The menu is the same at both locales and features Injaian's creative variations of Near Eastern and Mediterranean dishes. At lunchtime, the popular quiches are still there, ranging from the classic Lorraine to spinach, mushroom or shrimp. There is also a fascinating "aram sandwich," of roast beef and cream cheese rolled in Armenian lovash bread. Moussaka, shish kebob, kibbeh and that most divine of Morrocan delicacies, bastilla—bits of chicken and almonds encased in layers of paper-thin, sugar-dusted pastry. Plates are lavishly garnished with fruits and cheese. (Lunches are $4 to $5.) Dinners at Caravansary are preceded by a platter of "meza," spicy Middle Eastern appetizers—mixed vegetable pickles, turnips pickled with beet juice, eggplant crushed with sesame seeds, puréed garbanzos, more. Coffees are freshly roasted and ground.

CARAVANSARY (MARINA), 2263 Chestnut Street, San Francisco. Telephone: (415) 921-3466. Hours: 11:30-3, 5-10, Monday-Saturday; Sunday brunch. Cards: AE, BA, MC. Reservations accepted for dinner only. Wine and beer only. Street parking.

CARAVANSARY (DOWNTOWN), 310 Sutter Street, San Francisco. Telephone: (415) 362-4640. Hours: 11-3, 5-10, Monday-Saturday. Cards: AE, BA, MC. Reservations accepted for dinner only. Full bar service. Parking in nearby garages.

Caravansary
DINNER

APPETIZERS

Smoked Salmon	1.50	Quiche	1.00
French Pâté Country Style	1.50	Soup of the day	1.00

CARAVANSARY DINNER

Meza - A selection of middle eastern cold delicacies
Tossed green salad, House dressing

ENTREES
Served with pilaf.

Chicken *(daily choice of one)*   **6.95**
> Geras – Boneless breast of chicken with wild rice, pine nut and raisin stuffing. Baked in a dark rum and cherry sauce.
> Tabaka – Boneless breast of chicken marinated in pomegranate juice, then pressed and baked in lemon butter, garlic and herbs.
> Tsi-Tsi Belli – Boneless breast of chicken baked in pomegranate sauce and crushed walnuts.

Lamb Shank   **5.95**
> Tender baby lamb shanks baked in tomato sauce and sherry.

Shish Kebab   **6.95**
> Choice cuts of lamb marinated with chopped onions, fresh ground pepper, salt and sweet basil. Broiled on a skewer with tomatoes, onions and bell peppers.

Brochette of Filet   **7.95**
> Choice filet cuts of beef mildly seasoned and broiled on a skewer with tomatoes, onions and bell peppers.

Broiled Fish   **7.95**
> Fish in season charcoal broiled and served with lemon butter and capers.

Roast Duck à la Setrak   **6.95**
> *Friday and Saturday*
> Succulent roast duck in a piquant orange sherry sauce.

Quiche   **4.95**
> Lorraine, Spinach, Mushroom or Shrimp. Served with soup or salad.

San Francisco: Downtown
CHEZ LEON
French Basque $$

Small, elegant and sophisticated, Chez Leon is one of our favorite downtown haunts for a leisurely lunch and, due to location, a good choice for a pre-theater dinner. Basque-born owners Jean-Marie Lagourgue (the maître d') and his brother Pierre (the chef) received their training at Paris' Ritz Hotel and Le Crillon. Luncheon entrées ($3.95 to $6.95) include a selection of omelets, sweetbreads sauté, and seafood. Dinners ($6.95 to $10.50) include soup, a delicious salad, dessert or fresh fruit. Among the entrées are filet of sole with capers and mushrooms, veal in piperade and sour cream sauce, sweetbreads financière, scallops sauté in white wine and mushrooms, medallion of beef with mushrooms and artichoke, and steak au poivre. Though often slow, the service is attentive and you really feel that they do care about you. And at the door when you leave, Jean-Marie will present you with a rose.

CHEZ LEON, 124 Ellis Street, San Francisco. Telephone: (415) 982-1093. Hours: 11:30-2:30, 5-10, Tuesday-Saturday. Cards: AE, BA, CB, DC, MC. Reservations essential for lunch, advised for dinner. Parking in downtown lots. Full bar service.

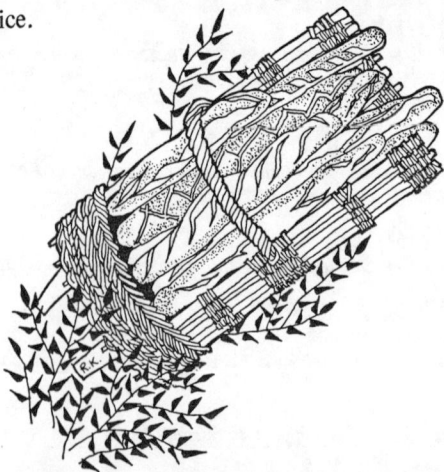

Dinner

SERVED WITH

**SOUP DU JOUR OR ONION SOUP GRATINÉ
SALAD PIERRE**

∽ *Entrées* ∽

CHOICE OF

FILET DE SOLE AUX CÂPRES OU BELLE MEUNIERE *6.95*
FILET OF SOLE WITH CAPERS OR WITH LEMON JUICE AND MUSHROOMS

ESCALOPE BISCAYENNE *8.95*
VEAL IN PIPERADE AND SOUR CREAM SAUCE

BROCHETTE DE CREVETTES PEYO *8.50*
PRAWNS SAUTE WITH TOMATO, GREEN PEPPER AND MUSHROOMS

ST. JACQUES DUGLÉRÉ *7.50*
SCALLOPS SAUTE IN WHITE WINE, TOMATO AND MUSHROOMS

RIS DE VEAU FINANCIÈRE *7.50*
SWEETBREADS, SAUCE FINANCIERE, MUSHROOMS AND OLIVES

ESCALOPE JEANNETTE *8.95*
VEAL AND MUSTARD AND SOUR CREAM SAUCE

MEDAILLON DE BOEUF MURAT *9.25*
BEEF WITH MUSHRQOMS AND ARTICHOKE

STEAK AU POIVRE *9.25*
PEPPERED FILET MIGNON SAUTE

SPECIAL DU JOUR *8.25*
ASK WAITER

Rack of Lamb (for two) 21.00

Desserts

CREME CARAMEL, GATEAU BASQUE, CHOCOLATE MOUSSE

or

FRESH FRUITS

Beverages

**COFFEE, TEA or SANKA
CAFE FILTRE *1.20***

San Francisco: North Point
CHEZ MICHEL
French

$$$

C'est très chic, from the pale ash paneling of the two dining rooms, the polished wood tables and the gleaming brass bar to the patchwork canopy which covers the ceilings in a riot of bold-patterned fabrics. Michel Elkaim has not overlooked a detail to please his sophisticated clientele. There is even a bidet in the ladies' room! Complete dinners on the facing page include soup or a salad of butter lettuce sprinkled with Roquefort, and dessert. Try the chocolate truffle cake—a sinfully rich wedge of fudgelike consistency. In addition to the dinners, there are another seven à la carte entrées, which include a house specialty of boneless trout stuffed with sorrel and beautiful white baby veal in a champagne sauce. But the tab can rise quickly if you order from this side of the menu: entrées are priced from $8.50 to $10.25; soups, salads and hors d'oeuvre average $3. Chez Michel is one of the few restaurants in the city where you can eat after midnight. A light supper menu is served from 11 to 1 am.

CHEZ MICHEL, 804 North Point, San Francisco. Telephone: (415) 771-6077. Hours: 5:30 pm-1 am, daily. Cards: BA, MC. Full bar service. Street parking or in Ghirardelli Square Garage.

Au Diner

La Salade ou La Soupe du Jour

Les Mets

Les Crêpes
Crêpe de Fruits de Mer
Sea Food

Crêpe A La Reine
Chicken and fresh sauteed mushrooms

Crêpe Florentine
Fresh spinach, cheese and spices

Two Crêpes — any combination   8.75

Le Pigeon Farci   11.50
Stuffed Squab

Le Poulet à la Périgourdine   9.75
Stuffed Chicken, Truffle Sauce

L'Entrecôte Bordelaise   11.50
New York Steak with Marrow and Red Wine Sauce

La Brochette de Filet de Boeuf   10.25
Beef Brochette with Bordelaise Sauce

Le Ris de Veau a l'Estragon   9.75
Sweetbreads in Tarragon Sauce

Le Médaillon de Bass Doria   9.75
Sea Bass Meuniere with Cucumbers

Le Filet de Sole Poché D'Antin   9.75
Poached Filet of Sole with Cream, Mushrooms, Tomatoes, White Wine

Les Noisettes d'Agneau   11.50
Filet of Lamb, Sauce Bearnaise

Café et Dessert

Chocolate Truffle Cake   Crème Caramel

Coupe Maison

San Francisco: Noe Valley
DIAMOND SUTRA
International $

This neighborhood restaurant is a tranquil setting for an informal dinner. The high-ceilinged room has whitewashed walls, long wooden benches and beautiful tables made from finely grained tree trunks. From the small open kitchen comes an amazing array of dishes from around the world. Owner Gladwin Solomon is from India and he usually prepares a few dishes from this cuisine—chicken Kashmir, perhaps, or curries. But you will also find a selection of Mediterranean foods: Moroccan or Greek lemon chicken, a Greek pie of spinach and phyllo dough, spinach and walnut lasagne, Italian mushroom casserole, asparagus or broccoli quiches make regular appearances on the nightly changing menu. There is apt to be a Chinese dish as well, or something from Latin America, and always several vegetarian entrées. Solomon and his helpers collect recipes and love to experiment. Dinners here ($4.50 to $4.95) include a freshly made soup, luscious salad and one of the finest molasses breads in town. Desserts are a forte as well. Swiss honey-walnut torte, chocolate praline log, pot de crème are but a few of the repertoire.

DIAMOND SUTRA, 737 Diamond Street, San Francisco. Telephone: (415) 285-6988. Hours: 6-10; closed Tuesday. No cards. No reservations. Wine and beer only. Street parking.

EDUARDO'S
Italian/Pasta $

Ask a San Franciscan where to go for fresh, homemade pasta and the answer you're most likely to get is "Eduardo's." In this inconspicuous "mama-papa" restaurant, Eduardo makes you feel glad you came and his wife prepares each dish to order from freshly made egg noodles. There are six styles of fettuccine, ranging from the classic white sauce version to a carbonara, containing bits of bacon and Parmesan cheese. Eduardo's also offers four variations of tortellini, the little pasta shells (made with plain egg paste and spinach paste), stuffed with a forcemeat of veal, beef, ham and mortadella. There is lasagna, cannelloni and five kinds of spaghetti. Eduardo's does have a small selection of meat and poultry dishes, but pasta is the real reason for coming here. And people do come in droves. Be prepared to wait. Pasta dishes are $4 to $4.75. Add a salad or a bowl of minestrone, and your bill will still be in the $5 range.

EDUARDO'S, 2234 Chestnut Street, San Francisco. Telephone: (415) 567-6164. Hours: 5-10, Tuesday-Saturday. No cards. Reservations not accepted. Wine only. Street parking.

San Francisco: Richmond District
EL MANSOUR
Moroccan

$$

There has been a recent explosion of Moroccan restaurants in San Francisco, all with similar menu, design and theme. El Mansour is one of the newer, one of the best and also the least expensive. The room exudes a rosy glow, from the lush Oriental rug on the floor to the silk-draped tentlike ceiling. Low, inlaid wooden tables are surrounded by hassocks and pillows. A waiter rinses your hands from a large brass bowl and pitcher in an ancient hand-washing ritual. Dinners here—feasts would be a better word—are a set price of $9.25 and begin with a spicy lentil soup. Next, three Moroccan salads of tomatoes, carrots and cucumbers are served, to be scooped up with pieces of Arabic bread. (No knives or forks here; everything is eaten with your fingers.) Then comes bastilla, a mound of paper-like pastry, dusted with powdered sugar, encasing slivers of chicken and almonds. For the main course (yes, another) there is a choice of Moroccan dishes—couscous, perhaps, or lamb, chicken or hare stewed with fruits, redolent with honey, lemon and Mideastern spices. For dessert, bananas fried with honey, and, of course, tea. El Mansour is owned by the Algerian-born Rouas brothers who also own two of the city's finest French restaurants: L'Étoile and Fleur de Lys.

EL MANSOUR, 3123 Clement Street, San Francisco. Telephone: (415) 751-2312. Hours: 6-10; closed Monday. Cards: BA, MC. Wine only. Reservations advised. Street parking.

Harira Soup
Salade Mohammed V
Bastela du Chef.

Couscous with Lamb.
Couscous with Chicken.
Chicken with Almonds.
Chicken with Lemon.
Chicken with Honey and Prunes.
Lamb with Almonds.
Lamb with Lemon.
Lamb with Honey.
Lamb with Prunes.
Lamb with Vegetables.
Lamb with Egg Plants.
Lamb with Onions.
Rabbit with Paprika.
Brochette Kabab.
Turkey with Almonds.

Dessert, King Hassan.
The a la Menthe.

Price 9.25

San Francisco: North Beach
EL MESON
Spanish $$

Hemingway fans might think they have been here before. One would almost expect to see Papa sitting at the bar discussing the last run at Pamplona. For El Meson ("The Inn") is very much like the inns of the Spanish countryside which he immortalized—whitewashed walls lined with art, wainscotings of dark-stained wood and tile floors. Taped music of Spain fills the room or occasionally a flamenco guitarist drops in. There is no prescribed Spanish cuisine, but rather each region of this culturally and geographically diverse country has its own specialties—the paella of the Levante, the chilindron sauces of Aragon, the zarzuela of Catalonia. The menu here, listing some 30 entrées, reflects this diversity. Seafood, so very popular in Spain, is highlighted here. You might try the zarzuela Costa Brava, a mélange of shrimp, scallops, squid, clams and white fish in a rich sauce laced with sherry. From northern Spain comes trucha a la Navarra, a most unusual rendition of trout, sautéed with serrano ham and covered with strips of sweet red pepper. There are several versions of squid; bowls of fresh clams steamed in white wine with lots of crunchy French bread for dunking up the juices; and prawns sautéed in oil and *mucho* garlic, recalling to memory the beaches of southern Spain. Dinner prices include either a hearty, homemade soup or salad with a garlicky dressing, and an outstanding creamy flan custard. The lunch menu is almost identical to dinner, but priced à la carte from $3.25 to $5.75.

EL MESON, 1333 Columbus Avenue, San Francisco. Telephone: (415) 928-2279. Hours: noon-3, 5-10:30, daily. Cards: AE, BA, MC. Reservations advised. Full bar service. Street parking or in nearby garage.

Dinner

~Pescados (Fish)~

Salmon a la Parrilla	Grilled salmon.	7.75
Trucha a la Navarra	Treut sauteed in cured Serrano ham and wine.	7.25
Filete de Lenguado Rebozado	Filet of sole breaded.	6.50
Bacalao a la Vizcaina	cod fish Bilbao Style	6.50

~ Mariscos (Seafood) ~

Langosta a la Parrilla	Grilled lobster. (For 2)	17.50
Langosta a la Termidor	Lobster thermidor. (For 2)	17.50
Paella Valenciana	Saffron rice paella with chicken, assorted seafood & vegetables.	7.50
Paella Marinera	Saffron rice paella of assorted seafood & vegetables.	7.50
Calamares Rebozados	Breaded baby squid.	5.75
Calamares Salteados	Sauteed baby squid.	5.75
Fritura Malagueña	Assorted fried seafood and shellfish.	6.50
Almejas a la Marinera	Fresh clams steamed in white wine.	7.25
Gambas a la Plancha	Prawns grilled on the shell.	7.50
Gambas al ajillo	Prawns sauteed with garlic and wine.	7.50
Zarzuela Costa Brava	Assorted seafood and shellfish.	7.25
Ostras al Mesón	Sauteed oysters in our house sauce.	6.75

~ Carnes (Meat) ~

Solomillo a la Pimienta	Filet mignon spiced with pepper.	8.50
Lomo de Cerdo	Loin of pork with sherry sauce.	7.25
Chuleta de Cordero	Lamb marinated and grilled.	7.25
Chuleta de Cordero a la Segoviana	Lamb chops. Segovian style	7.50
Ternera a la Parrilla	Grilled veal steak.	7.25
Ternera con Champiñones	Veal with mushrooms and cream sauce.	7.75
Filete de Añojo	N.Y. steak in sherry sauce with mushrooms and pimientos.	7.75
Pollo Chilindrón	Chicken sauteed in serrano ham, tomatoes, wine & pimientos.	6.25
Pollo al Jerez	Chicken style Jerez	6.25
Pollo al ajillo	Chicken with garlic sauce.	6.25

Includes Soup or Salad, Rice, Vegetables, Flán & Coffee.

San Francisco
Richmond District and the Cannery
EL SOMBRERO
Mexican

$

For some three decades El Sombrero has been serving Mexican food of uncompromising quality with portions of enormous quantity. The original locale, out on Geary Street, has a hacienda look with whitewashed walls, heavy wooden furniture, wrought-iron detail. A newer branch at the Cannery has even more atmosphere from south of the border, a picturesque view of the Cannery courtyard, and mariachi musicians on Friday and Saturday nights. Rival restaurateurs have tried to copy El Sombrero's superb green chile sauce, but none can duplicate it. Do try the enchilada verde with this sauce, topped with sour cream. The chicken and avocado tostada is spectacular here, looking as beautiful as it tastes. Tacos burst with mounds of shredded chicken or beef. And even the tortillas are freshly made on the premises. Plates are priced from $2 to $5.75. There is an inevitable wait for a table at these popular spots.

EL SOMBRERO (RICHMOND DISTRICT), 5800 Geary Boulevard, San Francisco. Telephone: (415) 221-2382. Hours: 11:45-10:30, Tuesday-Thursday; 11:45-11:30, Friday and Saturday; 1-10:30, Sunday. No cards. Reservations not accepted. Full bar service. Street parking.

EL SOMBRERO (THE CANNERY), 2801 Leavenworth, San Francisco. Telephone: (415) 474-6314. Hours: 11:45-10:30, Tuesday-Thursday; 11:45-11:30, Friday and Saturday; 11:45-10:30, Sunday. Cards: AE, BA, DC, MC. Reservations not accepted. Full bar service. Validated parking in Cannery lot.

San Francisco: Sunset District
EL TOREADOR
Mexican

$

Few American restaurants adventure into the unusual regional cooking of Mexico. At El Toreador it is a welcome relief from the usual taco/enchilada combination plate. (They have those here, too.) From owners Gonzalo and Carmen Garcia's native Guadalajara come sopes, a thick corn tortilla pressed with chorizo sausage. The chicken mole here is superb, the bittersweet chocolate sauce spiced with chile; also the enchilada mole. Chile verde combines cubes of pork in a mild sauce of orange juice, green pepper, onions and tomatoes. Or, for the adventurous palate, eggs scrambled with cactus. The small dining room has been spruced up with wooden beams, wrought-iron woodwork and a wood wine bar. Dinners are reasonably priced from $3 to $5 and include a soup seasoned with cilantro, plus beans, rice and salad. El Toreador suffered a setback in 1976 when the Garcias were briefly in Mexico, but all is well here again.

EL TOREADOR, 50 West Portal Avenue, San Francisco. Telephone: (415) 664-9800. Hours: 11:30-9, Monday-Thursday; 11:30-10, Friday; 4-10, Saturday; 4-9, Sunday. Cards: BA, MC. Reservations not required. Beer and wine only. Street parking.

San Francisco: Chinatown
FAR EAST CAFE
Chinese

$

The garish, neon-lit exterior looks like another Grant Avenue tourist trap, but inside it's old Chinatown revisited. Magnificent ornate Chinese lanterns are suspended from the ceiling and diners are seated in the privacy of curtained booths at tables covered with starchy white cloths. There is an extensive Cantonese menu here with all the classics such as tomato beef, beef with oyster sauce, prawns with black bean sauce, with most dishes priced in the $3 to $4 range. The Far East prepares a superior family banquet with a day's notice for a table of 10. The banquet seating is upstairs, however, in a large room lacking any charm. Service at this old-time cafe is efficient, but one often has the feeling that Westerners are still regarded with some suspicion.

FAR EAST CAFE, 631 Grant Avenue, San Francisco. Telephone: (415) 982-3245. Hours: noon-3, 4-10; closed Wednesday. No cards. Reservations accepted for banquets only. Full bar service. Parking at Portsmouth Square Garage.

San Francisco: Richmond District
FIVE HAPPINESS
Chinese

$

When Chinese cooking teacher William Yang opened the first Five Happiness on Clement Street, his culinary talent attracted a loyal clientele despite the lackluster surroundings of his storefront cafe. Now Yang has opened a second Five Happiness on Geary, in larger quarters which are both more comfortable and more ornate. "Chinese kitsch" might be a better word for the red-and-gold lacquered panels, tasseled lanterns and plastic covers on the red-brocade chair cushions. But the food of northern and western China served here is obviously the work of a master chef. The menu offers a choice of over 100 dishes, with few priced above $4. These range from the hot and spicy specialties of Szechwan and Hunan to the milder foods of the North. Yang's hot and sour soup is one of the richest and best-balanced versions in town. His mu she pork, wrapped in paper-thin pancakes, is superb. Any dish with pickled cabbage is a good bet. But, in fact, so is anything on the menu.

FIVE HAPPINESS, 4142 Geary Boulevard, San Francisco. Telephone: (415) 387-2626. Hours: 11:30-9:30, Monday-Friday; 11-10, Saturday and Sunday. Cards: BA, MC. Reservations accepted. Wine only. Street parking.

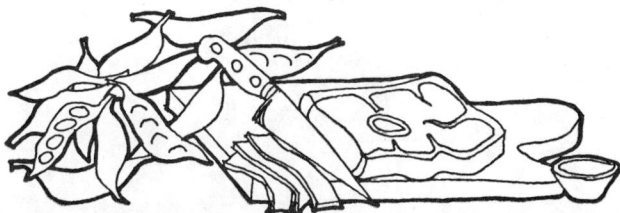

FLEUR DE LYS
French   **$$$**

Fleur de Lys is less formal and less expensive than the city's other top-flight French restaurants. And even though the printed menu is also more limited than its peers, Fleur de Lys will prepare any classic French dish if requested in advance. The interior, by designer Michael Taylor, resembles the tent of a rich sheik, with hundreds of yards of red and gold paisley cascading from a canopied ceiling to cover the walls. Dinners are à la carte here, but entrées are accompanied by potatoes and a vegetable. For appetizers try the gutsy, garlicky country-style pâté or cold asparagus with a heavenly mustard sauce, and for dessert the fresh strawberries over zabaglione when in season. The rack of lamb is a delight and the veal dishes are good. Owner/hosts are Maurice Rouas and his brother Claude, who is also a partner in L'Étoile.

FLEUR DE LYS, 777 Sutter Street, San Francisco. Telephone: (415) 673-7779. Hours: 6-11; closed Monday. Cards: AE, BA, CB, DC, MC. Reservations advised. Valet parking. Full bar service.

Entrées

L'Escalope de Veau à la Pointe du Bois 9.25
Veal in Truffle Sauce

L'Escalope de Veau au Champagne   8.25
Veal in Cream, Champagne Sauce

Le Piccata de Veau aux Courgettes 7.75
Veal Scaloppini with Zucchini

Le Carré d'Agneau Favorite 9.75
Roast Rack of Lamb

Les Côtes d'Agneau Grillées 9.00
Broiled Lamb Chops

Le Filet d'Agneau en Chemise (for two) 11.50 per person

Le Filet de Boeuf en Croûte (for two)10.25 per person
Filet of Beef in Pastry Shell

Le Steak au Poivre Flambé 9.75
Pepper Steak

La Brochette de Boeuf, Béarnaise 8.25
Tenderloin Tips of Beef

Les Tournedos de Boeuf Brigitte 10.50

Les Filet de Sole en Papillote Bonne Femme 7.25

Les Filets Rex Sole Belle Meunière 6.75

La Sole de la Manche, Véronique 8.75

Les Cuisses de Grenouilles Provençale 7.00
Frog Legs Sautées with Garlic

Les Ris-de-Veau Sauté au Madère 6.75
Sweetbreads in Madera Wine

Le Coq au Vin Rouge 6.75
Chicken in Casserole

La Poitrine de Volaille Archiduc 7.25
Breast of Chicken in Cream Sauce

Le Suprême de Volaille à l'Estragon 7.00
Breast of Chicken, Tarragon Sauce

Le Canard aux Figues 8.25
Duckling with Figs

San Francisco: Ghirardelli Square
GAYLORD
Northern India $$

With the opening of Gaylord in late 1976, the subtly seasoned cuisine of northern India reached San Francisco—by way of London, Chicago and New York. Gaylord is part of an international chain originating in New Delhi, which sends Indian chefs to the far-flung branches to make sure the authentic dishes are properly prepared. Each of the 50 menu items has its distinctive seasoning, ranging from mild to spicy, but none overly hot. Meats and breads charcoal-cooked in the clay-lined tandoori ovens of Punjab are the specialty, but there is a wide selection of sautéed, deep-fried and sauced dishes as well. To simplify ordering there are three preplanned dinners which provide a balanced introduction to north Indian food. But the more adventuresome diner might want to order an à la carte variety, sharing dishes Chinese-style. For four we would recommend the paprika-seasoned chicken tandoori, the lamb pasanda, prepared in a mildly seasoned cream sauce, a spicy prawn dish cooked with green peppers and onions, and a vegetable selection. Add to this a platter of assorted deep-fried Indian snacks (samosa, pakora, papadum), a bowl of outstanding mulligatawny soup, some of the side dishes like raita (vegetables in mint-flavored yogurt) or a refreshing cucumber salad, and for certain, the tandoor-cooked breads. You will have a feast indeed. Gaylord's dining room blends East with West by mixing potted palms, Indian paintings and artifacts with tables set with pink cloths and sparkling silver. Large windows offer views of the bay and Ghirardelli Square.

GAYLORD INDIA RESTAURANT, Ghirardelli Square, San Francisco. Telephone: (415) 771-8822. Hours: 11-3, 6-11, daily. Cards: AE, BA, MC. Full bar service. Reservations advised. Parking in Ghirardelli Garage.

TANDOORI

SPECIALTIES FROM THE CHARCOAL CLAY PIT

TANDOORI CHICKEN   Full **6.50**   Half **3.75**
Chicken marinated in yoghurt and roasted on skewers in clay pit

CHICKEN TIKKA KABAB   **4.50**
Boneless chicken pieces marinated and roasted on skewers in clay pit

BOOTI KABAB   **4.50**
Cubed leg of lamb roasted on skewer — spiced mildly

FISH TIKKA KABAB   **4.50**
Fish pieces marinated and roasted in the Tandoor

SEEKH KABAB   **4.50**
Minced lamb mixed with onions and herbs and spices, roasted on skewers

TANDOORI FISH   **6.00**
Whole fish marinated and roasted on skewers over charcoal

TANDOORI MIXED GRILL   **6.00**
Assortment of Tandoori specials

TANDOORI JUMBO PRAWNS   **6.50**
King prawns spiced and roasted in the Tandoor

GOSHT LAZIZ

LAMB SPECIALTIES — CURRIED

ALOO GOSHT   **4.90**
Curried lamb cooked with potatoes

ROGAN JOSH   **4.90**
Most popular lamb dish

LAMB PASANDA   **4.90**
Boneless lamb chunks cooked in mildly spiced cream sauce with nuts

SAG GOSHT   **4.90**
Lamb cooked with spiced cream spinach

NARGISI KOFTA   **4.90**
Minced lamb meat balls stuffed with egg in a succulent gravy

San Francisco: Financial District
GOLDEN EAGLE
Continental $$

Each prix fixe dinner at the Golden Eagle reflects the masterful flare of chef John Hadley, who combines the unique and unusual with the traditional. Co-owner and host George Patterson may suggest entrées like lamb with anchovy sauce; steak embellished with aged cheddar cheese and/or red wine sauce; beef vinaigrette cooked in white wine, shallots, capers and a dash of dry mustard; or succulent prawns imaginatively prepared with horseradish, wine, lemon juice and a dab of orange marmalade. These and other equally stunning creations make dining at the Golden Eagle, whether at lunch with financiers or at dinner with friends, a golden experience.

GOLDEN EAGLE, 160 California Street, San Francisco. Telephone: (415) 982-8831. Hours: 11:30-2:30, 5:30-10, daily. Cards: AE, BA, MC. Reservations advised. Full bar service. Parking in nearby garage.

Fisherman's Prawns
Marinated—then broiled.

Broiled Beef Roll
Stuffed with Italian seasoning.

Hunter's Stew
A combination of chicken, veal & beef.

Chicken Devine
Breast, gratiné with broccoli.

Casserole of Crab
Served on a bed of spinach.

Chicken San Joaquin
Sauté with olives, tomatoes & mushrooms.

Fresh Sand Dabs
Sauté—when available.

Sautéed Scallops
New England's best.

Beef Vinaigrette
Boiled Beef with our own sauce.

Front Street Steak
Stuffed chopped sirloin.

Escalopes of Veal
with mushrooms & vermouth.

Curry of Shrimp
Served on a bed of rice.

Sheepherder's Lamb
Marinated, skewered, & broiled.

New York Steak
$2.00 extra.

Oysters Nabob
Broiled with bacon.

Sweetbreads Supreme
With mushrooms & cream.

Soups of the Day

Caesar Salad
Mixed Green Salad
Hearts of Romaine
(with Bleu Cheese)

Pecan Pie
Coeur a la Creme
Monterey Jack Cheese
Caramel Custard
Chocolate Rum Mousse
Cheese Cake
Our Own Ice Cream
Frozen Orange Soufflé

San Francisco: Richmond District
HAHN'S HIBACHI
Korean $

You may initially be surprised to find gas-fueled hot plates as table centerpieces in this small friendly restaurant, but once you experience the culinary delights they create, your reservations will be dashed. Korean-style barbecue is the basis of the enthusiasm here; barbecue choices ($4.25 to $7) range from beef, pork, chicken, shrimp and scallops to beef intestine. All are first marinated in a mixture of soy sauce, sesame oil, wine, garlic, ginger, sugar, sesame seeds and pepper; then they are brought to the tables on a plate with yellow and green onion pieces and mushroom slices. The waitress slides the mixture onto a shallow cast-iron cooking vessel and cooks it over the high flame of the hot plate. Try the pork with hot sauce, delicately seasoned chunks of fresh-tasting scallops, or the spicy beef intestines, which are unbelievably rich in flavor. Large, meaty barbe-cued short ribs are brought to the table already cooked. Dinner begins with a bowl of subtly seasoned broth and a cold "relish plate" of cooked spinach with sesame seeds and bean sprouts, steamed rice, and a bowl of kim chee, a Korean relish. For an appetizer try the jeon, slices of a variety of vegetables, oysters, liver, ground beef, etc., indi-vidually dipped in egg and lightly fried; or one of the raw fish dishes: cuttlefish, octopus, tuna or abalone. Jung-gol, broth dishes of meat and vegetables, are also served, but the emphasis here is definitely on the barbecue dishes.

HAHN'S HIBACHI, 2121 Clement Street, San Francisco. Telephone: (415) 221-4246. Hours: noon-10 pm, daily. Cards: AE, BA, CB, DC, MC. Reservations recommended. Beer and wine only.

San Francisco: Chinatown
HUNAN
Chinese (Hunan) $

This might not be the best Chinese restaurant in the United States, as a *New Yorker* writer recently proclaimed, but eating at the tiny Hunan is an experience unlike any in San Francisco. The midblock locale on Kearny Street is the definitive "hole in the wall." Five small tables are crammed into a room, devoid of embellishment, with a counter along one side behind which the food is cooked. (Sit here for a fascinating close-up of the chefs at work.) At this writing plans were underway to open a larger branch on Sansome Street. But it is the food which is important. Here Henry Chung has introduced San Franciscans to the spicy, smoky, garlicky cuisine of his birthplace, the province of Hunan in southwestern China. You might start your meal with crackling, deep-fried onion cakes, made with eggs and scallions, or with plump dumplings filled with spiced meats and vegetables. Do try one of the salads, too: a fiery combination of shredded chicken, cucumber and noodles or a milder hot and sour concoction of mashed eggplant—refreshing and delicious. Smoked dishes are a specialty of Hunan: There is a choice of smoked ham, chicken or duck, cooked with bamboo shoots, onions, hot peppers and fresh garlic. Pork comes in a number of versions: Our favorite is the steamed spareribs, coated with fragrantly seasoned rice flour. And for dessert, there are sweet rice dumplings with fermented rice wine. A party of four can dine here fabulously and spend little more than $5 each.

HUNAN RESTAURANT, 853 Kearny Street, San Francisco. Telephone: (415) 788-2234. Hours: 11:30-3, 4:30-9:30, Monday-Friday; closed weekends. No cards. Reservations not accepted. Beer only. Parking in nearby garage. New branch location at 924 Sansome Street to open in the summer of 1977. Hours are the same as Kearny Street, except that it is closed on Monday and Tuesday and open on weekends.

San Francisco: Cow Hollow
KICHIHEI
Japanese $$

To the Japanese the appearance of food is as important as its taste. In this artistry Kichihei Ohara excels. As you enter his unobtrusive Chestnut Street restaurant you pass by a small counter, behind which Mr. Ohara deftly slices and cooks, arranging each plate as if it were a work of art. Beyond this is a small, simply furnished dining room with traditional low tables and tatami mats on one side, Western seating on the other, and windows looking out to a Japanese garden. There is a broad spectrum of dishes from which to choose. In addition to perfectly prepared tempura, sukiyaki and teriyaki dishes, there is shabu-shabu, nabemono (meal in a pot), shioyaki (salmon broiled in salt) and an exquisite sashimi, with the paper-thin slices of tuna arranged like petals of a large flower. For a side dish, don't miss the nasu-shigiyaki (eggplant broiled with a sweet bean sauce). Complete dinners here with salad, soup, rice and dessert are $4.95 to $5.95; nabe dishes are $3.25 to $4.10 à la carte. But for a truly distinctive meal we recommend you splurge, place your trust in Mr. Ohara and order the omakase ryori ($7.75), a multiple-course authentic Japanese dinner which includes many delicacies unknown to most Westerners. (Advance reservations required.) Wines here are limited to Sebastiani jug wines, but sake and Japanese beers are available.

KICHIHEI, 2084 Chestnut Street, San Francisco. Telephone: (415) 929-1670. Hours: 5-10, Monday-Saturday; 4:30-9:30, Sunday; closed Wednesday. Cards: AE, BA, CB, DC, MC. Reservations advised. Wine and beer only. Parking in public lot on Pierce Street between Chestnut and Lombard.

kichihei dinners

salad   soup   rice   dessert
included with dinners

a.
tempura and
sukiyaki   5.95

b.
tempura and
chicken teriyaki   5.25

c.
sashimi and
sukiyaki   5.25

d.
sashimi and
tempura   5.35

e.
tempura and
beef teriyaki   5.95

f.
sashimi and
chicken teriyaki   4.95

g.
sashimi and
beef teriyaki   5.25

h.
sashimi and
salmon teriyaki or
salmon shioyaki   5.50

i.
tempura and
salmon teriyaki or
salmon shioyaki   5.95

San Francisco: Richmond District
KHAN TOKE
Thai

$$

Standing amidst the storefronts of Geary Street in the Avenues is this outpost of Thai cuisine. Its nondescript exterior gives no hint of the beautifully executed interior: a small dining room done in warm, rich reds with windows extending across the back wall overlooking a garden. You will be seated at low tables, with floor cushions and bolsters as your seating. To enjoy the most comprehensive dining experience come as a party of six: The menu lists a complete dinner at $7.95 that offers a choice of two entrées from a selection of 12; eat family style and everyone in your party will have a chance to taste the wide array of flavors and textures possible here. Dinner begins with a light deep-fried fish cake of ground carp, egg and minced vegetables. The beef salad combines onion, tomato, cucumber and paper-thin slices of pink beef, dressed with lime and chili; the egg salad is lettuce, onions, pieces of hard-cooked egg white with a delicate yolk-based sauce drizzled over the top. The soup, available in a spicy or mild version, is a lemony broth with shrimp, tomato chunks, straw mushrooms and coriander leaves. Spicy and mild beef curries, Thai-style barbecued chicken, batter-dipped prawns, satae (grilled pork or beef accompanied with peanut sauce), chicken with herbs and slices of green chili, fried rice noodles and white fish in a hot pepper sauce are some of the entrées available, all served with steamed rice. Dessert is canned tropical fruits or fresh ones, such as papaya, when available. Enjoy an icy cold Thai beer with your dinner.

KHAN TOKE, 5937 Geary Boulevard (at 24th Avenue), San Francisco. Telephone: (415) 668-6654. Lunch: 11-3 (different menu available). Dinner: 5-11. Closed Monday. Cards: BA, MC. Reservations recommended. Beer and wine only.

San Francisco: Japantown
KOREA HOUSE
Korean $

A new location with a pleasantly decorated dining room has replaced the down-at-the-heels look of the original one (just a couple of doors down), but the good, full-flavored Korean food served here has been left intact. Try the bulkoki, tender marinated beef slices, or one of the marinated beef intestines preparations popular with the Koreans. Dak-bokkoom-almond chicken produces no almonds, but the succulent chunks of chicken prepared with vegetables (carrots, onions, zucchini, asparagus) in a spicy-hot sauce with a sweet edge is very good. Also recommended are the raw fish dishes—tuna, abalone—and the squid dishes, especially a "sautéed cuttlefish" with vegetables. Dinners are accompanied with a clear broth, kim chee, sesame-seasoned bean sprouts and cold cooked spinach. Also recommended are the buckwheat noodles with meat, eggs and vegetables and the meat dumplings in beef broth. Some of the tables have built-in braziers for at-the-table cooking of many of the dishes on the menu. Prices average $4.50 to $5.

KOREA HOUSE, 1640 Post Street, San Francisco. Telephone: (415) 563-1388. Hours: 11:30 am-3 am, Tuesday-Sunday. Cards: BA, MC. Reservations not necessary. Full bar service. Street parking.

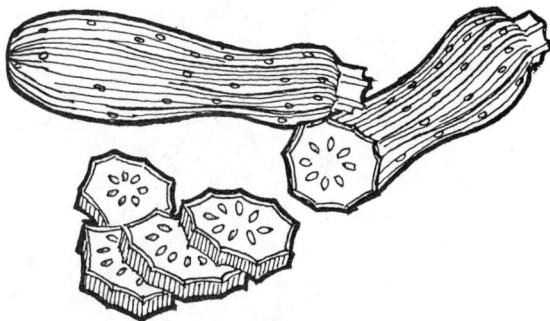

LA MIRABELLE
French

$$$

For years La Mirabelle has been a reliably good French restaurant, but when chef Jean Barlerin took command of the kitchen, the food soared to superlative. If awards were given for courageous menus (distinctive, but not widely popular selections), La Mirabelle deserves first prize for its appetizers. There are calf's brains sautéed in butter and capers, calf's tongue ravigotte, bone marrow, mussels in season and one of the world's lightest versions of quenelles. Chef Barlerin also prepares a truly great mushroom salad and an outstanding country pâté. In addition to the dishes described on the menu, Barlerin enjoys preparing any classic French dish a customer wishes, providing the ingredients are on hand and the kitchen is not too busy. Owners Fritz Frankel and Alfred Obermayer supervise the dining room where the service is formal, yet friendly. There is a comfortable bar and a long narrow dining room decorated in flocked paper and fleurs de lys.

LA MIRABELLE, 1326 Powell Street, San Francisco. Telephone: (415) 421-3374. Hours: 5:30-10:30, Tuesday-Saturday. Cards: AE, BA, CB, DC, MC. Reservations advised. Full bar service. Valet parking.

Nos Spécialités

Scampis à la Facon du Chef . . . 8.75
Genuine Langoustines Sauté in Garlic Butter

Medaillons de Veau Murat 9.75
Filets of Veal with Artichokes and Mushrooms

Emince´ de Veau a'la Crème . 8.25
Sliced Filet of Veal in Cream Sauce

Carré d' Agneau Provencale (2) . . 22.75
Rack of Lamb

Saumon Poché Beurre Nantais · · · 8.50
Fresh Poached Salmon in Season

Brochette de Boeuf aux Herbes . . . 8.75

Barquette de Fruits de Mer 9.50
Fresh Seafood

Ris de Veau au Madére 8.50
Sweet Breads

Médaillons de Boeuf Marchand de Vin 9.75

Filet de Veau Petit Palais (for 2) . . 21.00
Filet of Veal in Cream Sauce

Entrées

Cotelettes d'Agneau Grillées Vert Pré . 9.25
Lamb Cotelettes

Prawns Creole au Pernod 8.75

Entrecôte au Poivre Vert 10.50
New York Pepper Steak

Poulet Grand Mere (for 2) 30 minutes 15.75

Filet de Sole Mirabelle 8.25
In Cream Sauce

Filet de Sole Grenoblois 7.75
Sole Meuniere

Rognon de Veau Mirabelle 8.25
Kidneys in Cream Sauce

San Francisco: Richmond District
LA MAISONETTE
French $$

La Maisonette means "little house" but a more apt name for this neighborhood bistro would be "littlest house." About a dozen tables and a service bar are crammed into an incredibly tiny room which opens into an even smaller kitchen. Don't be alarmed to see three Chinese cooks at work there. The food is decidedly French, the recipes of Belgian-trained owner Leon Sedilla, who in turn trained his Chinese helpers before opening another restaurant, La Terrasse, in Palo Alto. The modestly priced dinners ($6 to $7.95), include a creamy soup, butter lettuce salad with a tart dressing, and a choice of entrée: filet of sole, sweetbreads, fresh salmon, chicken in white wine, veal piccata and a superb vol au vent of sweetbreads in a puff pastry shell. La Maisonette is popular and crowded. If you have to wait, do so at the bar around the corner where you will be called when your table is ready.

LA MAISONETTE, 315 8th Avenue, San Francisco. Telephone: (415) 387-7992. Hours: 5-10, Tuesday-Saturday. No cards. Reservations advised. Wine only. Street parking.

San Francisco: North Beach
LA PANTERA CAFE
Italian $

For 60 years La Pantera has been pleasing North Beach diners at the same locale. And little has changed here except the addition of marbleized formica to the big tables, and a giant color photograph of Joe Alioto and his "all-American family" among the Italian travel posters that decorate the high walls of old-style pressed metal. Chic Telegraph Hill dwellers rub elbows with bohemian types and Italian old-timers at the big family-style tables. Everyone talks with everyone else and shares from the giant tureen of delicious fresh soup and platters of food that follow. The pasta course here is always extra-special (no meatballs and spaghetti); perhaps manicotti with an outstanding pesto sauce or ravioli with herb sauce, and there's always plenty for seconds. The main course is usually hearty and simple—big slabs of juicy roast beef or chicken, sometimes fish on Friday—and is accompanied by fresh vegetables, bowls of mashed potatoes and perhaps stuffed eggplant or frittata. Lastly a bowl of crisp greens is served with cruets of vinegar and oil and a platter of fruit and cheese. All this costs $6.50 and includes a small bottle of nondescript red wine. Come early; it's always packed.

LA PANTERA CAFE, 1234 Grant Avenue, San Francisco. Telephone: (415) 392-0170. Hours: 6-10, Tuesday-Saturday; 5:30-10:30, Sunday. No cards. No reservations. Full bar service. Street parking.

San Francisco: North Beach
LITTLE JOE
Italian $

Don't let the lunch-counter atmosphere here put you off. Devoted, in-the-know San Franciscans claim Little Joe serves some of the best Italian food in town—honest, unpretentious and cooked right before your eyes. It's culinary theater to watch the veal quick-sautéed for scaloppini. A specialty here is caiucco, a cioppino-like concoction of fresh seafood cooked with homemade tomato sauce. Chicken livers, tongue, petrale sole, even the humble hamburger on French bread are all superb. All with vegetables, cooked al dente. The crowd is a cozy mixture of North Beach and Pacific Heights, accommodating enough to move down a seat when a twosome comes in. This is primarily a luncheon spot, but the same menu serves an early dinner. Entrées are priced $3 to $4.

LITTLE JOE, 325 Columbus Avenue, San Francisco. Telephone: (415) 982-7639. Hours: 11-7:30; closed Sunday. No cards. No reservations. Wine and beer only. Street parking.

San Francisco: Cow Hollow
LA PERGOLA
Italian

$$

Within a year of its opening in 1975, this small Chestnut Street restaurant was being acclaimed as one of the top Italian dinner houses in town. But this came as no surprise to the cognoscenti. Co-owner and host is Luciano Maggiora, long-time maître d' at the Blue Fox, and his waiters are as disciplined and professional as one might expect. His partner Angelo Piccinini is one of the best Italian chefs around. Particularly recommended here is the veal in lemon sauce, the saltimbocca and an exceptional chicken vecchia usanza, sauced with white wine, artichoke hearts, mushrooms and zucchini. Pasta is also first-rate and the selection is broad: spaghetti carbonara or al pesto, gnocchi, exceptional tortellini (from the same source as that served at the Blue Fox) and a classic fettuccine Alfredo made with the freshest of noodles. La Pergola, meaning grape arbor, is aptly named. The entire ceiling of the small dining room is covered by an arbor, through which light filters from above–a sort of eternal summer twilight. Prices here are all à la carte and a three-course dinner (splitting a salad and pasta) will be around $10 per person. Wines are highly priced, too.

LA PERGOLA, 2060 Chestnut Street, San Francisco. Telephone: (415) 563-4500. Hours: 5-10:30, Monday-Saturday. Cards: AE, BA, MC. Reservations advised. Wine and beer only. Street parking.

ANTIPASTI

SHRIMPS UMBERTO . . . . . . 2.50 *(bay shrimps, baked)*		ANTIPASTO ITALIANO 2.25	
PROSCIUTTO & MELONE 3.00		SHRIMP COCKTAIL 2.25	
ARTICHOKES VINEGRETTE 1.75		SCAMPI DELLA CASA . . . . . . 2.95 *(baked)*	
TOMATOES . . . . 3.00 *(w/bay shrimps & hearts of palm)*		ESCARGOTS 3.50	

PASTA

CANNELLONI ROMANA 3.75	FETTUCCINE ALFREDO 4.00	
SPAGHETTI CARBONARA 4.00	LINGUINE ALLE VONGOLE 4.00	
TORTELLINI ALLA PANNA 3.75	RAVIOLI DELLA CASA 3.50	
GNOCCHI LUCCHESE 3.50	TORTELLINI BOLOGNESE 3.75	
SPAGHETTI AL PESTO 3.50	SPAGHETTI BOLOGNESE 3.50	
LINGUINE ALLA NAPOLETANA . . . 3.50		

SPECIALITÁ

SCALOPPINE DI VITELLO ALLA PERGOLA 6.25

SCAMPI ALLA MEDITERRANEO 6.25

SWEETBREADS SAUTE (w/sherry & mushroooms) . . 5.75

EGGPLANT PARMIGIANA 4.50

VITELLO ALL'AGRO DI LIMONE 6.00

PICCATA DI VITELLO CON CARCIOFINI 6.50

CHICKEN VECCHIA USANZA 5.50

FILET OF SOLE AMANDINE 5.00

SALTIMBOCCA ROMANA 6.25

POLLO ARROSTO CON SALVIA 5.00

ABALONE (w/sauce meuniere) 7.75

NEW YORK CUT SIRLOIN 7.25

BUON APPETITO

In Pane Vita — In Vino Verita

San Francisco: Mission District
LA TRAVIATA
Italian

$$

A scruffy block of Mission near 24th may seem an unlikely place to find a superior Italian restaurant. But in the kitchen of this modest storefront restaurant, Sicilian-born Gaetano Ramaci turns out a wide variety of pasta, veal, chicken and seafood dishes, masterfully seasoned and expertly prepared. In the comfortable, candlelit dining room his partner Zef Shllaku is an amiable host to a growing clientele from all parts of town. Entrées here are accompanied by a fresh vegetable, like sautéed red peppers, and a generous portion of exquisite pasta—a choice of spaghetti or ravioli with an incredibly fresh tomato sauce, or an outstanding tortellini, bathed in a delicate cream sauce. Among our favorites here are chicken La Traviata with a superb mushroom sauce, a particularly piquant veal piccata, calamari with fresh tomatoes and mushrooms, a garlicky gamberoni (large prawns) and one of the lightest gnocchi around. Of the à la carte side dishes we recommend splitting an order of the antipasto which includes a small tart green salad. Soups have disappointed. Desserts are first-rate Italian pastries from Dianda's bakery next door.

LA TRAVIATA, 2854 Mission Street, San Francisco. Telephone: (415) 282-0500. Hours: 4-11; closed Monday. Cards: BA, MC. Wine only. Reservations advised. Street parking.

A LA CARTE

SPECIALTIES

LASAGNA (baked in individual casseroles) 3.75
CANNELLONI (ricotta, spinach & meat sauce) 3.75
EGGPLANT PARMIGIANA (baked with marinara sauce) 3.75
GNOCCHI (potato dumplings with tomato sauce) 3.75
TORTELLINI ROMANA (filled noodles in cream sauce) 3.75
LINGUINE & CLAMS (baby clams sauté with pasta) 4.00

VEAL

SCALOPPINE (mushroom sauté) 5.25
MILANESE (breaded veal cutlet) 5.25
PIZZAIOLA (garlic & butter sauté with marinara) 5.25
MARSALA (browned in butter & marsala wine) 5.25
PICCATA (capers, lemon, butter & white wine) 5.25
PARMIGIANA (baked with cheese & tomato sauce) 5.50
LA TRAVIATA (served with tortellini alla romana) 5.50

CHICKEN

AL FORNO (baked in butter & sherry) 4.00
FIORENTINA (boned & fried in special seasoning) 4.00
SAUTE SEC (fresh mushrooms & white sauce) 4.50
CACCIATORA (mushrooms, bell pepper, wine & tomato) 4.50
LA TRAVIATA (boned & sauté with mushrooms on rice) 4.50
(PLEASE ALLOW 25 MINUTES)

FISH

FILET OF SOLE (sauté in lemon butter sauce) 4.25
CALAMARI (squid sauté in tomato & butter sauce) 4.25
SCALLOPS (browned in sherry & butter) 4.75
GAMBERONI (large prowns in wine, lemon & butter) 5.25

BEEF

NEW YORK STEAK (pan fried with touch of garlic) 7.00
GROUND ROUND STEAK (with mushrooms) 4.25
STEAK SANDWICH AL PIATTO (small new york) 4.25
(ALL ENTREES SERVED WITH VEGETABLES
AND A CHOICE OF SPAGHETTI OR RAVIOLI)

San Francisco: Nob Hill
LE CLUB
French $$$

Tucked away in a corner of the Clay-Jones apartment building atop Nob Hill, Le Club is one of the city's best-kept secrets. They do absolutely no advertising and their loyal local clientele isn't talking either. Yet strangers are treated as royally as the once-a-week regulars. The two small dining rooms on either side of the comfortable mahogany bar are elegantly appointed with red velvet draperies, velvet-covered chairs, gold-rimmed china and flowers. Of the two, the "gold room" is preferable; it is smaller, quieter and free of the kitchen traffic that crosses the mahogany-paneled "red room." One of Le Club's impressive touches is the personalized matches that are on your table when you are seated. The menu is à la carte. Of the appetizers we like the prawns sauté in garlic and a delicate crêpe filled with curried shrimp (each $3.75). Except for lobster, the seafood is all fresh here, and the veal is Eastern. Fresh vegetables prepared with imagination and soufflé potatoes accompany the entrées. Some of our favorites are the saddle of lamb with chestnut purée and the duckling in Cointreau. But one of the best ways to approach the menu here is to let Bryan, the maître d', do the ordering for you. Chef Guy Grenier will prepare almost any classic French dish not on the menu by special request, too. He is noted for his dessert soufflés, which must be ordered when you make your reservation.

LE CLUB, 1250 Jones Street, San Francisco. Telephone: (415) 771-5400. Hours: 5:30-12; closed Sunday. Cards: AE, BA, MC. Reservations required. Full bar service. Coat and tie or turtleneck requested. Valet parking.

Malasol Caviar 13.50   Strasbourg Foie Gras 7.50   Prawns Sauté 3.75.
Escargots Bourguignonne 4.00.   Curried Shrimp Oriental 3.75.
Bay Shrimp Cocktail 3.75.   Oysters Imperial 4.00.

Belgian Endive & Watercress 3.75   Salade Le Club 3.75.   Limestone Lettuce 3.75.
Wilted Spinach 3.75.   Salad Matrimonial 3.75.   Caviar pour-deux 6.00.

Broiled Rock Lobster Tails ~ drawn butter 13.50.
Filet of Sole ~ sautéed in butter with mushrooms 8.50.
Frog Legs Provençal 9.50.   Sole Véronique 8.50.   Poche Salmon Hollandaise 8.50.
Crisped Duckling at Cointreau 9.50.   Breast of Chicken with Cognac & Pfifferlinge 8.50.
Beef Tenderloin Béarnaise for Two 25.00.
Individual Rack of Lamb 12.00.   Saddle of Lamb & Chestnut Purée 13.50.
White Veal Sauté Le Club 9.50.

Breast of Capon with Cognac & Chestnuts 8.50.
Sweetbreads in white wine sauce with mushrooms and Truffles 9.00.
Émincé of Veal aux Chanterelles 10.00.   Entrecote with Cépes and Cognac 12.50.
French Lamb Chops & Mint 10.00.   Tournedo Rossini 11.00.   Steak aux Poivres with Flambé 12.00.

61

San Francisco: Richmond District
LE CYRANO
French   **$$**

This is one of the most popular of the neighborhood French restaurants. And it has a very "neighborhood" feeling about it, as if the same people are returning, night after night. Owners Bernard Bovigny and Jacques Gaiddon have studiously avoided the "candlelight and roses" cliché of so many French restaurants in this country and, as is done in France, provide decent overall lighting so that you can see what you are eating. Tables covered with white cloths are set close enough together so that you can chat with your neighbor if you're in the mood. For an incredibly reasonable price ($5 to $9), you are served a four-course, classic French dinner. The luscious cream soups, usually watercress or leek and potato, get you off to a notable start. The salad is butter lettuce. Of the 15 entrées, one of our favorites is the rack of lamb, encrusted with garlic and parsley. The sweetbreads in a light cream sauce are outstanding. The veal is tender though of the Western variety. For a finale there is a choice of cheese or six desserts.

LE CYRANO, 4143 Geary Boulevard, San Francisco. Telephone: (415) 387-1090. Hours: 5-9:30; closed Sunday. No cards. Reservations advised. Full bar service. Parking in French Hospital lot across the street.

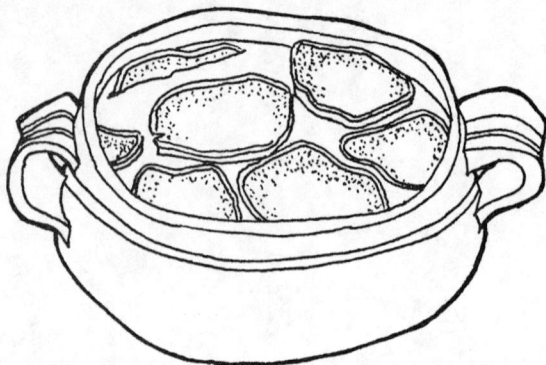

DÎNER

Soupe à L'Oignon Gratinée ou Potage du Jour

Salade des Quatre Saisons

SOLE DU PACIFIQUE COLBERT **$7.00**
Deep Fry Rex Sole

COQUILLE ST. JACQUES NORMANDE **7.00**
Baked Scallops and Shrimps Cream Sauce

CUISSES DE GRENOUILLES PROVENÇALE . . . **6.95**
Frog Legs Sautéed Garlic Butter

OMELETTE "FROMAGE OU CHAMPIGNONS" . . . **5.00**
Cheese or Mushroom Omelette

POULET SAUTÉ CÔTE D'AZUR **6.00**
Chicken Sautéed in wine

POULET DU DAUPHIN **6.25**
Chicken Sautéed, Cream and Mushroom

MIGNONNETTES DE VEAU BERGERAC **6.95**
Thin Slices of Veal Sautéed

MEDAILLONS DE VEAU DU CHEF **7.15**
Veal Sautéed, Cream and Vermouth

RIS DE VEAU LAVALLIÈRE **6.75**
Calf's Sweetbread, Wine and Cream

BOEUF EN DAUBE BEAUNE VILLAGE **6.10**
Beef Sautéed in Burgundy Wine

CÔTES D'AGNEAU VERT PRÉ **7.10**
Broiled Lamb Chops

CARRÉ D'AGNEAU PERSILLÉ **9.00**
Rack of Lamb

BROCHETTE DE FILET HUSSARDE · . . . **7.00**
Grilled Tenderloin of Beef on Skewer

TOURNEDOS HELDER **8.75**
Filet of Beef Bearnaise and Tomato

CONTRE FILET GRILLÉ AU POIVRE · · . . **8.75**
Peppered New York Steak

FROMAGE
OU
CRÈME RENVERSÉE — MOUSSE AU CHOCOLAT
PÊCHE ROXANE — POIRE BELLE HELENE
GLACE — SORBET

San Francisco: Nob Hill
L'ÉTOILE
French

$$$

Located in the exclusive Huntington Hotel atop Nob Hill, L'Étoile inspires such adjectives as elegant, chic, sophisticated. It has, to many, the finest French food in San Francisco and without a doubt, the most civilized bar ... small, romantically lit, with a New York air and a piano player who knows Cole Porter. A wide staircase leads down to the elegant dining room with French latticework, enormous urns of fresh flowers, sparkling silver and crystal, a few tables interspersed with the curved banquettes. Service is impeccable under the scrutiny of one or the other of the two owners, Henri Barberis, who came here via the famous New York Pavillon, or Claude Rouas, who once worked at the equally demanding Maxim's in Paris. Complete dinners (opposite page) are $17. There is also an extensive and expensive á la carte menu with entrées in the $9 range and vegetables extra. The dessert soufflés are fabulous.

L'ÉTOILE, 1075 California Street, San Francisco. Telephone: (415) 771-1529. Hours: 5:30-11, Monday-Saturday. Cards: AE, BA, CB, DC, MC. Reservations required. Full bar service. Valet parking.

Menu du Dîner

Pau Piettes de Sole

Crêpes Maxim's

Barquette de Crevettes Joinville
Marinade d'Hareng au Vin Blanc

Pâté Maison

Melon Bayonne

Salade Maison ou Potages

Potage du Jour

Soupe à l'Oignon Gratinée

Consommé Chaud

Vichyssoise Froide

Saint-Germain

La Soupe de Poisson

Entrées

La Poulette A' L'orange
Roast Cornish Hen, Wild Rice

Le Caneton aux Pêches
Roast Duckling

La Poitrine de Volaille Farcie Perigourdine
Stuffed Breast of Chicken

Les Grenouilles Provencale
Frogs' Legs Sautées

Les Délices de Sole Normandie
Poached Filet of Sole

La Rex Sole Meunière
Rex Sole Sautée

Les Quenelles Maison Cardinal
Mousse of Bay Fish with Lobster Cream Sauce

L'Escalope de Veau au Champagne
Scallop of Veal in Champagne

L'Escalope de Veau Cordon Bleu
Stuffed Veal, Ham & Cheese

Mignonette d'agneau a La Chartres
Filet of Lamb sauteed in Taragon Sauce

Les Brochettes de Bœuf Béarnaise
Tenderloin Tips of Beef

Le Grenadin de Bœuf Grand Mère
Médallions of Beef and Wine Sauce

Les Ris de Veau Sautés Grenobloise
Sweetbreads Sautées

Desserts au Choix

Pêche Melba

Crème Caramel

Oeufs a la Neige

Glaces: Vanille, ou Chocolat

Tarte Maison

Poire Hélène

Parfait aux Marrons

Cheese Cake

Sorbet au Citron

Café   Thé   Lait   Sanka

65

L'ORANGERIE
French $$$

Despite a string of Holiday awards, L'Orangerie has had its ups and downs in recent years, mainly due to the service. At this writing it's way up, close to the top of San Francisco's roster of posh French restaurants. The rise has been due, primarily, to the presence of Hans Brandt, the city's *premier* maître d' who for years presided in the Captain's Cabin of Trader Vic's. L'Orangerie is decidedly a "special occasion" restaurant and its atmosphere bespeaks its namesake: the greenhouse at Versailles. Latticework covers the walls of the springlike dining room; orange topiaries are set about; the candlelit tables are set with flowered serving plates. Dinners here are á la carte. One of the more unusual appetizers are the quenelles, the fish dumplings bathed in a tarragon and clam sauce rather than the traditional sauce Nantua. One of our favorite main dishes is the porc L'Orangerie, a roast loin cooked in a sauce of oranges and brandy. The veal here is of exceptional quality for San Francisco, usually pearly white and fork tender. Dessert soufflés—chocolate or Grand Marnier—are a forte of the chef. (The portion is large; you might ask for one order split for two.) Or you might want to ignore all the preceding suggestions and ask Hans to order for you. That is his forte. With its O'Farrell Street location, L'Orangerie is an excellent choice for a post-theater supper, when they have a special menu for $8 per person.

L'ORANGERIE, 419 O'Farrell, San Francisco. Telephone: (415) 776-3600. Hours: 5:30-12:30, Monday-Saturday. Cards: AE, BA, DC, MC. Reservations advised. Full bar service. Valet parking.

QUENELLES DE POISSON A NOTRE MANIERE	3.75
a fish mousse, with a clam sauce,	
our specialty served as a main course . . .	8.00
SAUMON POCHE SAUCE MOUSSELINE	
ou	
SAUMON GRILLE	9.50
TURBOT POCHE SAUCE HOLLANDAISE . .	10.50
imported french turbot when available	
SOLE DU PAS-DE-CALAIS MEUNIERE . . .	9.75
imported french sole	
CANARD A L'ORANGERIE . . . . for two	20.50
at least 35 minutes	
FAISAN EN SALMIS PERIGOURDINE . for two	24.00
pheasant & goose liver	
LE COQ EN PATE . . . . , for two	21.50
our specialty, with goose liver and truffles; 25 minutes	
POUSSIN ALPHONSE . . . . , . .	9.75
with cream and truffles; 25 minutes	
CARRE OU SELLE D'AGNEAU FORESTIERE . .	11.50
with french forest mushrooms; 25 minutes for two or four	
FILET DE PORC EN CHEVREUIL . . . ,	9.50
in a game sauce, when available	
CARRE DE PORC A L'ORANGERIE . . .	7.50
our pork specialty, with orange and cognac	
MEDAILLON DE VEAU MEDERIC	10.25
cream and mushrooms	
NOISETTE DE VEAU "LUR-SALUCES" . . .	10.25
flown in, milk fed veal, our creation	
POULET ROTI CRESSONNIERE . . . (for two)	17.00
ENTRECOTE BORDELAISE OU FINES HERBES . .	11.75
favorite french beef cut	
STEACK AU POIVRE CHEF ALPHONSE . . .	12.25
with pepper, cream and cognac	
TOURNEDOS ROSSINI	12.25
TOURNEDOS GRILLE BEARNAISE . , . .	12.25

San Francisco: Ghirardelli Square
THE MANDARIN
Chinese (Mandarin) $$

Mandarin cooking refers not to a specific region of China, but encompasses the finest foods from all areas as they were served to the emperors in Peking. At The Mandarin restaurant Madame Cecilia Chiang first introduced the total spectrum of Chinese *haute cuisine* to Californians. In addition to the subtle intricacies of the better-known Cantonese tradition, there are the peppery hot dishes of Szechwan and Hunan, the delicate seafood of Shanghai, the firepots and barbecues of the Mongols. The setting befits a Mandarin, too. An exposed-beam ceiling emulates ancient temple architecture. There are family paintings from Shanghai, Chinese rugs, Taiwanese tiles and a glimpse of the bay through narrow windows. In addition to the complete dinners, there is an extensive à la carte menu. But the best way to dine here is to organize a group of six or eight, call a day or so in advance and ask the restaurant's advice in planning a special banquet. This way you can sample some of the specialties like Mandarin duck, beggar's chicken baked in clay, shark's fin soup and the Mongolian firepot which require 24 hours' notice. And if you are truly interested in the culinary arts of China, don't miss Madame Chiang's Tuesday cooking classes. For $25 a session, you receive instruction in preparing three dishes, followed by an elaborate multi-course banquet, accompanied by wine and the stimulating conversation of Madame Chiang. (Classes limited to 12 persons, advance reservation required.)

THE MANDARIN, Ghirardelli Square, San Francisco. Telephone: (415) 673-8812. Hours: noon-midnight, Monday-Friday; 12:30-midnight, Saturday and Sunday. Cards: AE, BA, CB, DC, MC. Reservations advised. Full bar service. Parking in Ghirardelli Square Garage.

MANDARIN SPECIALTIES

(One day advance notice required)

MANDARIN DUCK
(Whole duck serves 4 or more)

Ours alone. And yours to relish. Prepared with prideful care
from our very own recipe originating from Peking itself!
Served with Chinese Pao-Ping, Scallions and Plum Sauce

21.00

CRISPY DUCK
(Whole duck serves 4 or more)

19.00

BEGGAR'S CHICKEN
(Whole chicken serves 4 or more)

The Mandarin takes great pleasure in being the first and only
Chinese restaurant in America, we believe, to serve this chicken
which is unusual in name. And in fact, unusual in presentation.
A fowl finely flavored, encased in clay, and baked

14.00

CRISPY CHICKEN
(Whole chicken serves 4 or more)

14.00

SHARK'S FIN SOUP
(Serves 4)

25.00

STUFFED CUCUMBER SOUP
(Serves 4)

7.50

San Francisco
Downtown and North Beach
MAMA'S
American $

It's hard to believe that the best lunch on Union Square is to be found in Macy's basement. But it's true. In a corner behind the gourmet cookware section is Mama's, an oasis of eternal spring with its latticework gazebo, potted flowers and hanging ferns. As you line up to place your order at the cafeteria-style counter, the abundance of fresh fruit salads and luscious pastries is awesome. Mama's also serves up a galaxy of omelets, French toast, several hot seafood or chicken dishes garnished with fruit, and a host of creative sandwiches like Charlie the Tuna (tuna and broiled tomatoes covered with melted cheese on an English muffin). Mama's original locale, looking out on Washington Square, still flourishes in North Beach and Sunday brunch here is a San Francisco institution of sorts. The menu and high level of quality is the same at both places. Recently Mama's opened a much larger and more formal restaurant at 1177 California Street on Nob Hill. You are served at the table here, and there is a dinner menu featuring Italian dishes. Somehow it lacks the appeal of her older branches. But it's good to know about if you are hungry after midnight; they serve until 1 am, Monday through Saturday.

MAMA'S DOWNTOWN, Macy's, Union Square, San Francisco. Telephone: (415) 391-3790. Hours: 9:30-7:30, Monday-Friday; 9:30-5, Saturday. Cards: AE. Reservations are only accepted a day in advance for parties of three or more; otherwise expect to wait in line. Wine only.

MAMA'S NORTH BEACH, 1701 Stockton, San Francisco. Telephone: (415) 362-6421. Hours: 8:30 am-8 pm, daily. No cards. Reservations not accepted. Wine only.

San Francisco: Downtown
MARIO'S
Mexican

$

Behind the nondescript facade is a little brick-walled dining room packed with candlelit tables jammed together. More tables are on a balcony above. Mariachi music from a blaring jukebox and the good smells of Mexican cooking fill the air. Dinners ($3 to $4.75) are served on enormous round platters, about a foot in diameter. Crispy shredded lettuce with tangy dressing, fluffy rice and refried beans topped with cheese accompany each order. Particularly good are the enchiladas suizas, filled with a mild cheese and covered with sour cream and a spicy red sauce. The chiles rellenos are encased in an exceptionally light batter. And the home-made corn-dough tamales, steamed in corn husks, are a delight. An unusual specialty here is machaca Sonorense, a sort of Mexican omelet containing shredded beef, bell peppers, onions and tomatoes. Steaks and sirloin strips are simmered in red or green sauces. We especially like to go here after 8 on Friday or Saturday night when there is a Mexican guitarist who plays and sings by request your favorite Mexican songs.

MARIO'S, 900 Bush Street, San Francisco. Telephone: (415) 776-4490. Hours: 11:30-11:30; until 12:30 weekends. Cards: BA, MC. No reservations. Wine and beer only. Validated parking at garage next door.

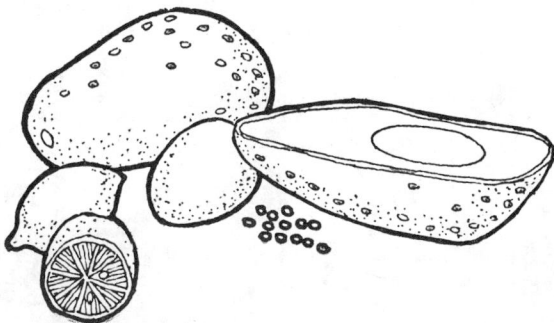

San Francisco: Ghirardelli Square
MODESTO LANZONE'S
Italian $$

There aren't too many restaurants where you'll find the owner around both at lunch and dinner, but Modesto is a born host, well known from his days at Vanessi's and later Julius Castle. There is no prettier spot in Ghirardelli for lunch than in the loggia room that overlooks the bay. Wicker furniture, terra cotta floors, pastel Oriental rugs and that magnificent bay! At night you're surrounded by the glittering lights of Ghirardelli. A long menu lists such Italian specialties as breast of capon rolled around ham and cheese, or breaded lamb chops. But it is in the pasta department that Modesto's is unexcelled. The fabulous agnolotti, rounds of dough stuffed with chicken then smothered in cream, superb cannelloni, fettuccine, gnocchi. With a spinach salad and the famous sacripantina cake, a perfect dinner. À la carte prices are shown on the opposite page; $2 more buys a complete dinner with soup or salad, pasta and dessert.

MODESTO LANZONE'S, Ghirardelli Square, San Francisco. Telephone: (415) 771-2880. Hours: noon-11, Tuesday-Saturday; 2-10, Sunday. Cards: AE, BA, CB, DC, MC. Reservations advised. Full bar service. Validated parking in Ghirardelli Square Garage.

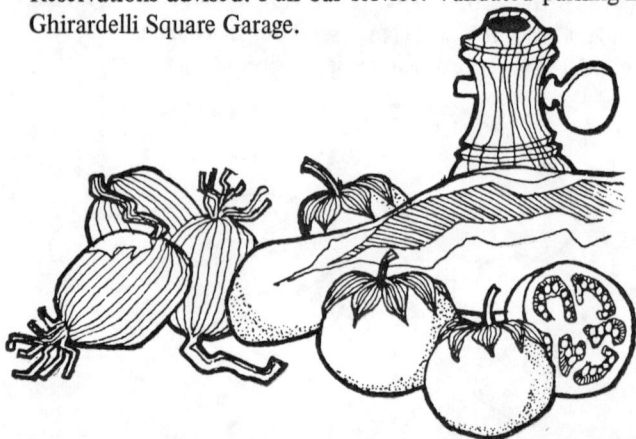

~∽~

AGNOLOTTI ALLA CREMA 4.75
    ROUND DISC OF PASTA STUFFED WITH CHICKEN, CHEESE AND PROSCIUTTO
LINGUINE MARINARA 3.95
    FLAT SPAGHETTI WITH TOMATO, OREGANO AND GARLIC SAUCE
FETTUCCINE AL PESTO 4.25
    NOODLES WITH BUTTER, BASIL AND CHEESE SAUCE
FETTUCCINE ALLA ALFREDO 4.50
    NOODLES WITH BUTTER, CREAM AND CHEESE
TORTELLINI ALLA VENEZIANA 4.50
    STUFFED PASTE WITH HAM, CHEESE, TOMATO, CREAM SAUCE
LINGUINE ALLE VONGOLE 4.50
    FLAT SPAGHETTI WITH CLAM SAUCE
CANNELLONI ALLA ROSSINI 4.75
    ROLLED PANCAKE STUFFED WITH VEAL, CHEESE AND VEGETABLE
PANSOTI ALLA CREMA DI NOCI STILE MANUELINA 4.75
    STUFFED PASTE WITH RICOTTA AND WALNUT SAUCE
RAVIOLI GENOVESE 4.50
    PASTE STUFFED WITH VEGETABLES AND MEAT
GNOCCHI VERDI AL SUGO 4.50
    PASTE MADE WITH POTATO AND FLOUR
GUANCIALI AL FUNGHI 4.75
    PILLOW OF PASTE WITH RICOTTA AND MUSHROOMS

~∽~

PEPERONATA CON VITELLO 5.75
    VEAL SAUTE WITH BELL PEPPER
GAMBERI ALLA MARINARA 6.75
    PRAWNS SAUTE WITH GARLIC AND TOMATOES
FILETTO DI PETRALE AI FERRI 5.25
    BROILED FILET OF PETRALE WITH BUTTER AND LEMON
MELANZANE ALLA PARMIGIANA 4.75
    EGG PLANT PARMIGIANA
SOGLIOLA DORATA CON MANDORLE 4.95
    FILET OF SOLE D'ORE WITH BUTTER AND ALMONDS
SCAMPI PESCATORA 9.25
    BABY LOBSTER TAIL SAUTE WITH SHALLOTS AND WINE
CALAMARI GENOVESE 5.25
    SQUID, DEEP FRIED
PETTO DI CAPPONE PARMIGIANA 5.95
    BREAST OF CAPON PARMIGIANA
PETTO DI CAPPONE FARCITO VALDOSTANA 6.95
    BREAST OF CAPON WITH ITALIAN HAM AND CHEESE
POLLO ALLA CACCIATORA (for two) 13.00
    CHICKEN HUNTER STYLE
POLLO GERUSALEMME (for two) 14.00
    CHICKEN WITH ARTICHOKE HEARTS, MUSHROOMS AND SOUR CREAM
POLLO CON LASAGNE 6.50
    CHICKEN WITH LASAGNE
FEGATO ALLA VENEZIANA 4.95
    LIVER VENETIAN
FEGATINI DI POLLO AL VINO ROSSO 4.95
    CHICKEN LIVERS SAUTE
ANIMELLE ALLA FINANZIERA 5.75
    SWEETBREADS SAUTE
COTOLETTA PARMIGIANA 6.95
    VEAL CUTLET PARMIGIANA
BAULETTO DI VITELLO AL PROSCIUTTO E FUNGHI 8.50
    SLICED VEAL FOLD WITH PROSCIUTTO AND MUSHROOMS
COTOLETTA MILANESE 5.75
    BREADED VEAL CUTLET
PICCATA DI VITELLO AL LIMONE CAPPERI 6.95
    SLICED VEAL SAUTE WITH BUTTER, LEMON, CAPERS
SCALOPPINE DI VITELLO 7.25
    SLICED VEAL SAUTE WITH MUSHROOMS AND WINE SAUCE
SALTIMBOCCA 7.50
    SLICED VEAL WITH ITALIAN HAM
ABACCHIO AL FORNO 8.75
    LAMB ROASTED ROMAN STYLE
BOCCONI AL MARSALA 8.25
    FILET, MARSALA SAUCE
CONTROFILETTO DI MANZO ALLA PIZZAIOLA 8.90
    SIRLOIN STEAK SAUTE WITH BELL PEPPER AND TOMATOES
CONTROFILETTO AL FERRI 8.90
    BROILED SIRLOIN STEAK

~∽~

NORTH BEACH RESTAURANT
Northern Italian

$$

Any culinary similarities between the North Beach Restaurant and Ristorante Orsi are not purely coincidental. Bruno Orsi, co-owner and chef at North Beach, is the brother and former assistant of Oreste Orsi of Orsi's. And he carries on the same fine tradition of Tuscan cuisine. This attractive restaurant has a spontaneous character, as if everyone in town decided to drop in at the same time. Lunch is pleasant here, not as crowded as the financial district restaurants, with the sunlight filtering down through high skylights. Complete dinners include a memorable antipasto tray that includes a fantastic marinated calamari, a mixed green salad with Italian dressing, pasta with a prosciutto sauce, the entrée, and spumoni, cheese or fruit. À la carte prices of the entrées are about $3 less; lunches are in the $5 range. North Beach does an excellent job on local fresh seafood; pasta is made fresh daily.

NORTH BEACH RESTAURANT, 1512 Stockton Street, San Francisco. Telephone: (415) 392-1587. Hours: 11:30-midnight daily; closed Thanksgiving, Christmas, New Year's. Cards: AE, BA, CB, DC, MC. Reservations advised. Full bar service. Valet parking.

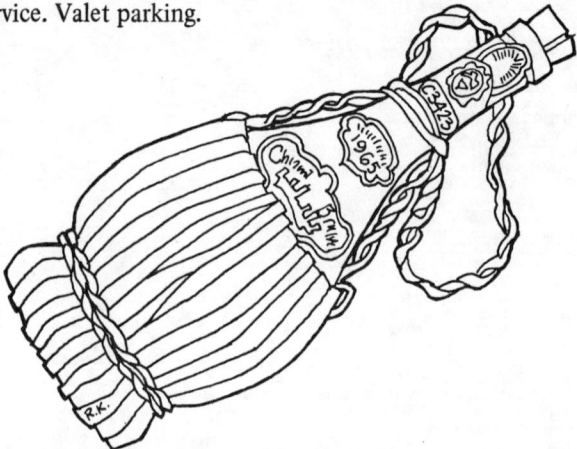

Entrees

All Entrees Cooked to Order and Served with Fresh Vegetable

Dinner includes antipasto

From the Sea

	Dinner
Calamari Livornese or Doré	7.70
Filet of Sole — Mugnaia	7.95
Filet of Sole — Almandine	8.70
Rex Sole Meuniere	8.70
Rex Sole Almandine	8.95
Sand Dabs from the Bay	7.95
Sand Dabs Almandine	8.70
Trout Mugnaia	8.70
Combination of Filet of Veal and Prawns	10.70
Roast Lobster Tail	13.25
Abalone Doré Mugnaia	11.25
Scampi Della Casa	11.25
Prawns Provinciale	9.70
Petrali Portofino	9.25
Salmon Steak Alla Perelli (in season)	9.75

From the Land

Egg Plant Parmigiana	7.50
Chicken Livers Saute with Mushroom Sauce	7.95
Sweetbreads Saute with Mushroom Sauce	9.50
Sweetbreads Supreme	9.50
Roast Caponette	7.70
Chicken Saute Toscana	8.70
Breast of Capon Valdostana	9.25
Chicken Al Mattone	8.25
Veal Scallopine Piccata Con Capperi	9.95
Veal Scallopine Pizzaiola	9.75
Veal Scallopine Supreme Alla Gina	9.75
Veal Scallopine All'Agro with Lemon Sauce	9.75
Veal Scallopine Marsala	9.25
Veal Milanese	9.50
Veal Scallopine All Bruno Con Pinoli	9.75
Veal Portafoglio with Grand Marnier Sauce	10.95
Veal Cutlets Parmigiana	8.50
Veal Scallopine Alla Valdostana	10.25
Lombatine Di Vitello Al Burro	9.75
Saltimbocca Alla Nerone	10.50
Roast Lamb Alla Bruno	8.95
Medallion of Beef	11.50
New York Steak	12.50
Filet Mignon	12.50
Steak Caruso	12.50
Beef Della Casa Al Canape for (2)	25.00

San Francisco: Financial District
ORSI'S
Northern Italian

$$$

Chef Oreste Orsi comes from Tuscany, source of Italy's finest cooking, and most local cognoscenti rate his subtle dishes the best northern Italian food in town. Orsi introduced cannelloni to San Francisco in 1957 and his version still reigns supreme. The other pastas, which are mostly homemade, are superb, too. Vegetables are fresh and cooked to order. If you splurge your way through the à la carte menu here, you could easily spend $20 per person. But if you are cautious and order only a salad and pasta or scaloppine, you could eat very well for under $10. Orsi's is extremely popular with businessmen for lunch and the service can be very slow. Dinnertime is less hectic. Orsi's partner Joseph Orsini is out front in the dining room.

RISTORANTE ORSI, 375 Bush Street, San Francisco. Telephone: (415) 981-6535. Hours: 11:30-11:30, Monday-Friday; 5-11:30, Saturday. Cards: AE, BA, CB, DC, MC. Reservations advised. Full bar service.

Killeen.

ANTIPASTI FREDDI

CHILLED TOMATO JUICE	1.25	CHILLED CLAM JUICE	1.50	RUSSIAN CAVIAR	7.50
CRAB COCKTAIL	4.00	CRAB LEGS ON ICE	4.25	PROSCIUTTO e MELONE	3.25
SHRIMP COCKTAIL	3.75	OYSTERS ON HALF SHELL (Blue Point)	4.25

FRESH ARTICHOKE, VINAIGRETTE .   . 3.50

ANTIPASTI CALDI

ESCARGOTS	4.00	SCAMPI SALTATI Mugnaia (for two)	10.50
ASPARAGUS alla "Orsi"	3.00	BAKED SHRIMP alla "Orsi"	4.75	OYSTERS alla "Orsi"	4.50
ALASKA CRAB alla "Orsi"	5.00

INSALATE

TOSSED GREEN SALAD	2.50	BELGIAN ENDIVE	2.75	CEASAR SALAD (for two)	7.00
LIMESTONE LETTUCE	2.75	SLICED TOMATOES	2.75	HEART OF PALM	3.00
HEART OF ROMAINE, ROQUEFORT	4.00	CHOPPED ROMAINE WITH SEA FOOD	5.00

MINESTRE

MINESTRA del GIORNO	1.50	TORTELLINI al BRODO	2.50	ZUPPA MARITATA	2.50

PASTA

CANNELLONI, RIPIENI	4.75	RAVIOLI CON SALSA	5.00	SPAGHETTI alla VONGOLE	5.50
TORTELLINI alla BOLOGNESE	4.75	SPAGHETTI, CARUSO	5.25	SPAGHETTI al DENTE	4.50
LASAGNE VERDI alla BOLOGNESE	4.75	FETTUCCINE alla ROMANA	4.75
TAGLIATELLE alla BOLOGNESE	5.00	FETTUCCINE (Champagne Sauce)	5.25

PESCE

BROILED LOBSTER TAIL	12.75	PETRALE, MUGNAIA	6.50	ABALONE STEAK	10.75
PETRALE, CARTOCCIO	7.00	LOBSTER THERMIDOR	14.00	SCAMPI SALTATI MUGNAIA	10.75

SPECIALITA

BREAST OF CAPON ALLA "ORSI"	7.00
BONED SQUAB STUFFED, Florentine	10.50
MEDAGLIONE OF BEEF WITH MUSHROOMS	10.00
SALTIMBOCCA ALLA FLORENTINA	7.50

BONED SQUAB STUFFED
Cherry Sauce 11.25
RACK OF LAMB, MINT JELLY   (FOR TWO) 24.00

PIATTI SALTATI

CHICKEN LIVER SAUTE	6.50	SCALOPPINE ALLA "ORSI"	7.25	SCALOPPINE ALL'AGRO	6.75
POLLO CACCIATORE	6.75	SCALOPPINE PICCATA	7.25	UCCELLETTI SCAPPATI	7.25
POLLO PAESANA, SECCO	6.75	VITELLA alla PARMIGIANA	7.25	BISTECCA DI VITELLA	10.50
				(Provimi)	

PIATTI ALLA BRACE

BROILED HALF SPRING CHICKEN	6.25	BROILED DOUBLE FRENCH LAMB CHOPS	10.75
BROILED WHOLE JUMBO SQUAB	10.50	NEW YORK CUT SIRLOIN STEAK	10.75
SPIEDINI DI FILETTO (Brochette)	9.25	FILET MIGNON	10.75
PAIARDA di VITELLA	6.75	DOUBLE NEW YORK CUT SIRLOIN (FOR TWO)	24.00
BISTECCA al MINUTO	9.50	TORNEDOES A LA "ORSI" (FOR TWO)	24.00
BISTECCA DI VITELLA, (Provimi)	10.50

San Francisco: Ghirardelli Square
PAPRIKÁS FONO
Hungarian   **$$**

Laszlo and Paulette Fono have a Midas touch with restaurants. Some years back they started making the palacsintas (crêpes) of their native Hungary in a little cafe that was the first of the now far-flung chain of Magic Pan Crêperies. The Fonos sold their interest in Magic Pan and invested in a dream: a first-class restaurant which offers a broad sampling of authentic Hungarian dishes as prepared in family kitchens and country inns. Since opening in 1974, Paprikás Fono has been a spectacular success. It does look like a Hungarian country inn—with a panoramic view of San Francisco Bay thrown in. Whitewashed walls are splashed with colorful pieces of hand-painted pottery and artifacts from Hungary. Leafy plants are everywhere and a flower-filled balcony overlooks the square and the bay. A house specialty is gulyas, the Hungarian herdsman's dish of chunks of beef and potatoes in a paprika-flavored broth; it may be ordered by the cup or by the kettleful as a meal in itself, accompanied by langos (a deep-fried bread rubbed with garlic), and a sweet cheese palacsinta. The selection of entrées is extensive, with some 15 offered at lunch and dinner. Portions are large and most dishes come with a salad of some type, such as marinated cucumbers. The exceptional butter lettuce salad is a good à la carte choice. The Fonos maintain their own bakery, where guests may watch the fancy tortes being prepared. The wine list specializes in the wines of Hungary with a smattering of California labels. The dinner menu is reproduced here. Lunches are under $4.

PAPRIKÁS FONO, Ghirardelli Square, San Francisco. Telephone: (415) 441-1223. Hours: 11:30 am-11 pm, Monday-Thursday; until midnight, Friday and Saturday; until 9:30, Sunday; closed Thanksgiving, Christmas, New Year's. Cards: BA, MC. Reservations advised. Full bar service. Parking in Ghirardelli Square Garage.

VEAL PAPRIKÁS
"Borju Paprikás". Tender pieces of veal in rich paprikás sauce. Served with our home made "Galuska" and cucumber salad. **$6.50**

HORTOBAGYI MIXED GRILL
"Fatanyeros". A combination of grilled meats common to the Hortobagyi Puszta (Great Plain). A beef fillet, skewered lamb, home made Debreceni sausage and grilled tender pork steak. Garnished with our peasant potato and red cabbage. **$8.95**

CHICKEN PAPRIKÁS
"Paprikas Csirke". Our version of this famous national dish. Boneless breast of chicken in a rich paprikás sauce with sour cream; served with our homemade "Galuska", and cucumber salad. **$6.25**

VEAL TOKANY
Tender veal cubes cooked in a delicate sauce with mushrooms and herbs. Served with "Tarhonya" and a tomato salad. **$6.50**

CASINO SUPPER
A meal reminiscent of dining in the days of the "National Casino." Fillets of chicken breasts, breaded and fried, garnished with our special potatoe in a cold piquant sauce. Served with a tomato salad. **$5.95**

MOTHER'S PALACSINTAS
Tender veal cubes cooked in delicate sauce with mushroom and herbs, folded in a palacsinta accompanied with our fluffy asparagus souffle palacsinta. Served with a green salad. **$4.95**

EGRI BEEF TOKANY
"Boros Tokany." Cubes of beef simmered in a delicately spiced redwine-mushroom sauce, served with "Galuska" and a tomato salad. **$5.75**

ESZTERHÁZY CHICKEN LIVERS
With a dash of herbs and red wine we rapidly saute chicken livers and mushrooms to capture their delicate flavor and texture. Served with "Tarhonya" and a green salad. **$5.95**

Vendéglő

The Vendéglő or "little restaurant" is found in towns, villages and cities throughout Hungary. Here one finds "family style" dining. Each has its own specialities reflecting the taste of the proprietor.

TISZA RIVER FISH PAPRIKÁS
"Rác Ponty." One of the most traditional ways of preparing this fresh water fish. A delicate fish fillet baked in rich paprikas sauce over scalloped potatoes. (Available in season only) **$5.25**

LAMB TOKANY
"Barany Tokany". Braised cubes of lamb slowly cooked in a savory sauce, served with "Tarhonya". A hearty meal. **$5.50**

LASZLO'S HEFTY PALACSINTAS
Three filled palacsintas that make a hearty dinner. A fried ham palacsinta, one light asparagus souffle and a third palacsinta with our fresh mushroom sauce. **$4.50**

ADRIATIC MEMORIES
Delicately flavored large shrimps grilled on skewers; served on a bed of fluffy rice with a shrimp and wine sauce. **$5.25**

Csárda

The "Csárda" or country inn was originally a haven for those on the road; from itinerant merchants and herdsmen to brigands and highwaymen. Even today its fare reflects those vanished, easy going times.

SHEPHERD'S GRILL
"Barany Nyarson." Marinated cubes of Lamb, with bacon and bayleaves grilled on skewers. Served with fluffy rice and a fresh mushroom sauce. **$5.25**

GYPSY STEAK
"Laci Pecsenye." Tender pork steaks seasoned with our special Hungarian seasoning and grilled in the manner of this nomadic tribe. Served with peasant potato and red cabbage. **$5.25**

TRANSYLVANIA CABBAGE GULYAS
"Székely Gulyás." Piquantly flavored diced pork and sour cabbage cooked in paprikas sauce. Topped with sour cream. **$4.95**

BANDIT'S GRILL
"Rablo Hus". Marinated chunks of beef and pieces of bacon grilled on skewers; served over a bed of rice with a fresh mushroom sauce. **$5.25**

From Our Gulyás Kettle

"GULYÁS" soup (Goulash) is one of the most famous Hungarian dishes. It is a hearty soup made with tender chunks of beef, diced potatoes simmered in a rich paprikas broth.

The name is derived from the world "Gulyá" meaning cattle herd. Since ancient times Hungarian herdsman the "Gulyás" have prepared their meals in the "Bogracs" a thin walled, portable iron kettle suspended over an open fire.

Here we cook the Gulyás in our bogracs, prepared the traditional way that we learned in our native Hungary.

CUP $.95   **KETTLE (Bogracs)** **$2.75**

San Francisco: Polk Street
RUE DE POLK
French $$

Polk Street's mixed bag of businesses—ethnic restaurants, gay bars, movie houses, hip shops and good food markets—attracts a cross section of San Francisco's many communities. But the street's tiny namesake restaurant is a quiet refuge from the bustle and hustle outside. It is peaceful and dignified, much like an unpretentious neighborhood restaurant in Paris. Behind the modest, cafe-curtained storefront, the dining room is simply and tastefully decorated with wood, flowers and soft colors. The chef and owner is Mike Caldwell, a former New Yorker who makes everything from scratch, even a superb vichysoisse—a rarity indeed in these days of convenience foods. His cooking does not aspire to the pinnacles of *haute cuisine,* but the food is reliably honest and bespeaks loving care in the kitchen. Prices are à la carte ($5.50 to $8.50) though a simply prepared fresh vegetable and rice or potatoes are included. The salad is fantastic, heaped with fresh grated Roquefort, and the chocolate mousse is outstanding. In fact, the appetizers and desserts here often surpass the main courses. The changing daily special is usually a good bet; if salmon is in season, Mike often serves it with a fine sauce mousseline.

RUE DE POLK, 2316 Polk Street, San Francisco. Telephone: (415) 441-0979. Hours: 6-11, Monday-Saturday. Cards: AE, BA, MC. Wine only. Street parking.

Appetizers

QUICHE LORRAINE	1.75	FINE LIVER PATE	2.00
STUFFED EGGPLANT	2.25	VEAL&HAM PATE EN CROUTE CUMBERLAND	2.50
	ESCARGOT DE BOURGOGNE	3.25	

Soups

MUSHROOM BISQUE	1.50	VICHYSSOISE	1.75
	ONION AU GRATIN	2.25	

Salads

MIXED GREENS with Vinaigrette Dressing and Choice of Avocado or Roquefort Garnish 1.50
SALADE MAISON, a large mixed greens salad with vinaigrette dressing, tomato wedges, egg halves,
      avocado slices, grated Roquefort and sliced mushrooms 4.00

Entrees

FILET OF SOLE AMANDINE served with Potato and Vegetables 5.50
    (Filet of Sole sauteed in butter with sliced almonds)

RED SNAPPER PROVENCAL served with Potato and Vegetables 5.75
    (Filet of Red Snapper cooked in sauce of Tomatoes, Shallots, Garlic, Parsley and Chicken Stock)

CHICKEN TARRAGON served with Rice and Vegetables 6.00
    (Chicken Breast and shallots in a white wine, chicken stock and cream sauce)

BEEF BOURGUIGNON served with Potato and Vegetables 6.25
    (Beef Cubes, mushrooms, onions, and carrots cooked in Red Wine)

LAMB BROCHETTE served on Rice with Vegetables 6.50
    (Lamb cubes, marinated in Red Wine, olive oil, herbs and spices)

VEAL FRANCHESE served with Potato and Vegetables 7.00
    (Veal Scallops, dipped in beaten egg and sauteed in butter with lemon slice)

SCAMPI THERMIDOR served with Potato and Vegetables 7.75
    (Baby Lobster Tails, flamed in Brandy and served in Thermidor Sauce)

STEAK DIANE served with Potato and Vegetables 8.50
    (Prime New York steak, flamed in brandy with a sauce of sherry, butter and chives)

FILET MIGNON MARCHAND DE VIN served with Potato and Vegetables 9.00
    (Broiled to order with a Demi-Glace and Red Wine Sauce)

Desserts

CREME CARAMEL	1.50	ICE CREAM WITH CHERRY HERRING	1.50
CHOCOLATE MOUSSE	1.75	RIZ a L'IMPERATRICE	2.00

Beverages

COLOMBIAN COFFEE, DARJEELING TEA, SANKA 50

San Francisco: Mission District
PABELLÓN ESPAÑOL
Spanish/Peruvian $

Walls covered with bullfight posters, plus flamenco guitarists on the weekends, make this crowded cafe *muy simpatica.* The specialties *de la casa* are the seafood dishes of Spain and Peru: There are several versions of shellfish stew, prawns in green sauce, steamed clams, squid, frogs legs and the classic Peruvian soup, parihuela. Half of the ocean's yield ends up in the paella Valenciana: crab, prawns, clams, squid, cod, as well as ham and chicken. For non fish eaters, there is marinated rack of lamb, bursting with flavor, and as an appetizer, Peruvian anticuchos, marinated and grilled hearts of beef. For an unusual dessert, try the teleme cheese with Argentinian sweet potato jam. Dinners are $3.50 to $5.75 with a lettuce-vegetable salad included.

PABELLÓN ESPAÑOL, 3115 22nd Street, San Francisco. Telephone: (415) 824-9852. Hours: 4-11; until midnight, Friday and Saturday; closed Tuesday. No cards. Reservations advised. Wine and beer only. Parking in lot next door.

San Francisco: North Beach
SAIGON ROYAL
Vietnamese $

Located on upper Grant amidst the constantly changing storefronts, this small, friendly place is popular with neighborhood residents. The large menu is divided into sections by price, from an incredibly low $2.50 to a top of $6, the latter being for a whole salt roasted crab (seasonal). Dinners begin with a rich chicken-rice soup with a slightly peppery flavor; crispy imperial rolls filled with pork, shrimp and vegetables or steamed rolls stuffed with mushrooms and pork make good appetizers. Chicken dishes are excellent here. Try the lemon grass, ginger or five-spice version. A popular dish is the crab shell stuffed with a well-seasoned mixture of crab meat, ground pork, vermicelli and vegetables; another favorite is the shrimp and pork brochette. There is also a variety of curries, the pork curry being especially good, and stir fries of chicken or pork with vegetables, and crab and chicken with vermicelli. Dessert is fruit—banana or pineapple—fried and sweetened with honey or sugar, and flamed at your table if you wish. Vietnamese noodle soups, lemon beef salad and other items are listed on a separate lunch menu.

SAIGON ROYAL, 1363 Grant Avenue (at Green), San Francisco. Telephone: (415) 397-7445. Hours: noon-10:30 pm, Monday, Wednesday-Saturday; 5 pm-10:30 pm, Sunday. Closed Tuesday. Cards: BA, MC. No alcoholic beverages. Parking difficult.

SAM'S GRILL
Seafood

$$

Don't be deterred by the corner saloon exterior. Inside you'll find old-fashioned, no-nonsense ambience with starchy white cloths, black-tied waiters and booths for private dining, usually occupied by financial district tycoons. You'll also find some of the best, freshest seafood in town. Our favorites are the boned rex sole, swimming in butter, and the steamed Alaskan cod. In nearly 30 years of dining here we've rarely been disappointed. The only problem is getting a table. Reservations are not accepted and you must arrive by 11:30 or come after 1 to get in for lunch. Dinner is not a problem, but they do close early. The à la carte menu is the same for lunch and dinner. The wines are extremely limited with only Almaden, Krug and Wente represented.

SAM'S GRILL, 374 Bush Street, San Francisco. Telephone: (415) 421-0594. Hours: 11-8:30, Monday-Friday; closed Saturday and Sunday. Cards: BA, MC. Reservations accepted only for parties of six or more. Full bar service. Parking in garage across the street.

FISH AND SHELLFISH

SPECIAL: Deviled Crab ala Sam 5.25
Fresh Salmon w Shrimp Creole or Newburg 5.25
Boned Rex Sole or Turbot ala Sam 4.15
Broiled Filet of Petrale 4.75
Fried Filet of Sole 3.75
Boned Sand Dabs ala Sam 4.25
Sam's Special Seafood Plate 6.50
Broiled Fresh Salmon 5.75
Steamed Alaska Cod 3.90
Fried Deep Sea Scallops, Tartar Sauce 4.90
Filet of Sole ala Marguery 4.50
Crab Creole or Curry with Rice 5.15
Shrimp Creole or Curry with Rice 4.50
Fried Crab Legs with Tartar Sauce 6.00
Crab Newburg 5.50
Abalone with Tartar Sauce 7.00
Fried Louisiana Prawns 6.00
Clams Elizabeth 5.25
Clams, Fried or Steamed 4.75
Shirred Eggs with Crab 5.50

TODAY'S SPECIAL FOR LUNCH

Baked Filet of Sole, Shrimp Sauce 3.25
Hamburger Steak, Tagliarini Mushroom 3.25
Tagliarini with Mushmroom Sauce 2.75
Crab Meat au Gratin 5.50
Baked Creamed Crab with Noodles 5.25
Shirred Eggs with Spinach Florentins.... 3.15
Cold Boiled Ham with Red Bean Salad 3.25
Breaded Veal Cutlet with Tagliarini
    and Mushroom Sauce 4.00
Fresh Mushroom Saute on Toast 3.25
Chicken Liver Omelette 3.25
Baked Macaroni with Chicken Livers ... 3.60
Salisbury Steak with Mushroom Sauce 3.75
    With Tagliarini and Parmesan 4.00
Alaska Cod with Scrambled Eggs 4.15
Boiled Salmon with Egg Sauce 6.00

San Francisco: Japantown
SANPPO
Japanese   **$**

Located across from the Japan Trade Center, Sanppo offers delicious dinners, from $3 to $4, which include a lacquered bowl of soybean soup, a small plate of crisp pickled vegetables, a large pot of rice and tea. There is a large selection of various meats and teriyakis, broiled and fried seafood and, for the more exotic palate, even barbecued eel over rice. There is also shabu-shabu, sukiyaki and a choice of nabe dishes (food served in a pot). The yosenabe is superb —a generous portion of oysters, clams, prawns, octopus, fish cake, pea pods, onion slices, bamboo shoots, Chinese cabbage, with a poached egg in the center and served with pongu, a lemon-flavored dipping sauce. No visit to Sanppo would be complete without ordering a side dish of gomaae spinach, prepared with sesame seeds and soy sauce. The tempura contains four enormous prawns and a generous serving of selected vegetables, perfectly done in a heavenly, crisp batter. For a quick lunch, the donburi (of which there are nine different kinds) are exceptional. Equally delicious and possessing the intriguing flavors of Japan are the nine different kinds of udon or soba (wheat noodles with broth, meats and vegetables).

RESTAURANT SANPPO, 1702 Post Street, San Francisco. Telephone: (415) 346-3486. Hours: 11:30-2, 5-10; closed Monday. No cards. No reservations. Sake and beer only. Street parking.

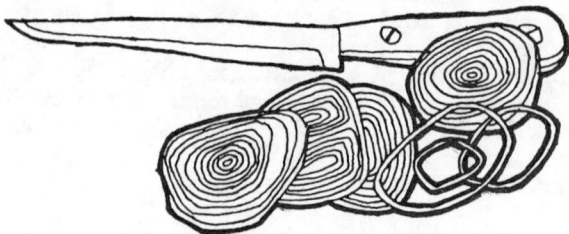

San Francisco: Japantown
SAPPORO-YA
Japanese

$

Sapporo-ya centers around two things—a large stainless-steel grill and homemade noodles. This is not to say only noodles are available here, but they are one of the main attractions of this small, pleasant place. The noodles are made of buckwheat flour and are either grilled (yaki) or served in broth (ramen). The soup noodles ($1.90 to $2.75) range from soy sauce ramen to various miso-based ramens: One of the best is miso cha-shu ramen, which features large thin slices of barbecued pork. It is delicious and will satisfy a trencherman's appetite. The grilled noodle dishes include beef and pork versions: thin slices of meat on a bed of lightly grilled noodles, bean sprouts and cabbage, dressed with a flavorful soy-based sauce and sprinkled with chopped green onions. These are reasonably priced at $2.30 and $2.20 respectively. Gyoza, half-moon dumplings filled with meat and minced vegetables, are also served. The teppan yaki dinners, prepared on the grill, include two beef selections, the meat tender and flavorful, and a shrimp and tofu combination. There are also several combination dinners ($4.65 to $4.95), featuring a variety of preparations: feather-light vegetable and shrimp tempura, a variety of sashimi, succulent chicken teriyaki on a bed of lightly grilled sprouts, beef teriyaki. All dinners are served with soup, sunomono (vinegared salad), rice, canned mandarin orange sections for dessert and green tea. À la carte dishes, including a pork cutlet with curry sauce, are also available. Portions are very large and moderately priced.

SAPPORO-YA, Japanese Cultural Center, 1581 Webster Street, No. 202, San Francisco. Telephone: (415) 563-7400. Hours: 11 am-2 am, Tuesday-Sunday. Cards: MC. Beer only.

San Francisco: Polk Street
SZECHWAN
Chinese (Szechwan)

$

The cooking of the tropical, southwestern Chinese province of Szechwan is characterized by the fiery fagara pepper which is used liberally to season many of the regional dishes. But not all Szechwanese cooking is hot. In their small restaurant, John and Helen Lee have introduced to San Francisco a number of dishes, both mild and hot, from their homeland. Even the hot dishes, however, may be ordered with less pepper, depending on the sensitivity of your palate. A pleasant contrast to the spicy dishes is Empress Tsu-Shi's shrimp, a mixture of shrimp, broccoli, ham, bamboo shoots and mushrooms in a creamy white sauce. The preserved ham, glazed with honey and cooked with lotus nuts, will add a sweet note to the balance of the meal. The whole cod, deep fried and coated with a very hot sauce, provides another contrast, as most of the other dishes are stir-fried. The Lees claim that the dishes listed on the facing page have never before been served in San Francisco. Included in these prices are an appetizer of spring rolls, soup and dessert. There are also some 30 additional dishes which may be ordered à la carte.

SZECHWAN RESTAURANT, 2209 Polk Street, San Francisco. Telephone: (415) 474-8282. Hours: noon-2, 5-10:30, daily. Cards: BA, MC. Wine and beer only. Street parking.

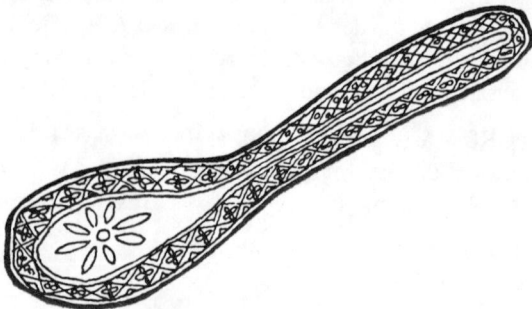

Szechwan Dinners

SLICED LEG OF LAMB, Szechwan Style   **5.95**
With choice Spring lamb with scallions and
hot pepper sauce

TA-CHIEN CHICKEN 5.50
Chicken chunks with tingling hot sauce.

EMPRESS TSU-SHI'S SHRIMP 5.95
Shrimp with broccoli, ham, bamboo shoots and
mushrooms in a white sauce. TSU-SHI was the
most powerful Empress in Chinese history.

CHENG-TU BEEF 5.50
Fillet of beef garnished with fresh Chinese
greens in a hot sauce.

O'MEI VEGETABLES 4.95
O'Mei is one of the four holy mountains of the
Chinese buddhist religion. Many people consider
the vegetarian dishes of O'Mei to be the best.

CHUNG-KING PRAWNS 5.95
Prawns sautéed in fresh garlic and ginger with
hot Szechwan sauce.

SZECHWAN LOTUS CHICKEN 6.50
Shredded chicken lightly sautéed with celery,
water chestnuts and mushrooms. This is
especially delicious rolled in lettuce.

LOBSTER SZECHWAN STYLE 7.95
An authentic Szechwan specialty. Delicate flavored
lobster sautéed in a unique Szechwan sauce.

HOT SPICY WHOLE FISH 7.95
Rock cod, deep fried, coated with hot spicy sauce.

FRESH PORK SZECHWAN STYLE 5.95
Sliced fresh pork sautéed in Szechwan red hot sauce.

San Francisco: Polk Street
SWAN OYSTER DEPOT
Seafood $

This little oyster bar is located in one of San Francisco's oldest fish markets. You're likely to see a chauffeured limousine pull up and the driver run in to pick up just-arrived East Coast oysters or perhaps the freshest of bay shrimp. Abalone, crab, clams, all are here just recently removed from their natural habitat. The counter has a dozen or so seats and serves lovely oysters on the half shell or a generous shrimp cocktail. You can feast on blue points for $2.50 the half dozen.

SWAN OYSTER DEPOT, 1517 Polk Street, San Francisco. Telephone: (415) 673-1101. Hours: 8 am-5:30 pm; closed Sunday. No cards. No reservations. Beer and wine only. Street parking.

San Francisco: Financial District
TADICH GRILL
Seafood

$$

Whether Tadich or Sam's serves the best seafood in town is a heated debate among San Franciscans and each camp has its staunch supporters. At both, however, the fish is the freshest available. Founded some 120 years ago, Tadich is the oldest restaurant in the city, though the owners and location have changed over the years. But the current site retains the turn-of-the-century atmosphere. At noontime the long lunch counter and intimate walnut booths are mobbed; arrive at 11:30 or after 1. Seafood entrées are $5 to $8.

TADICH GRILL, 240 California Street, San Francisco. Telephone: (415) 391-2373. Hours: 11:30-8:30; closed Sunday. No cards. No reservations. Full bar service. Parking in nearby garages.

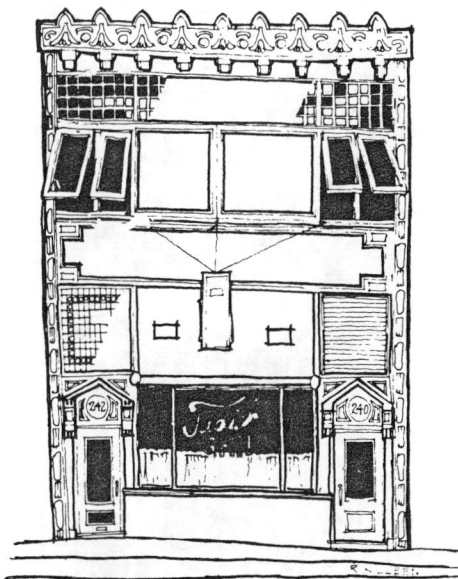

San Francisco: North Beach
TOMMASO'S
Italian (Neapolitan)

$$

Pizza was introduced to San Francisco, back in the 1930s, from the giant oak-burning ovens of this friendly and informal cafe, then known as Lupo's. Very little has changed over the years, except the name (which honors Lupo's long-time chef, Tommy Chin—who is Chinese!) and the ownership, now in the hands of Agostino Crotti who greets the guests with all the charisma of his native Italy. The pizza here, 19 varieties, is still the best in town (the calzone, a "pizza turnover," is sensational). But we prefer to order the Neapolitan specialties. You might start with platters of broccoli, string beans and toasted peppers marinated in oil and lemon (order several and share) or coo-coo clams baked in olive oil and garlic, spiked with chili peppers and Italian herbs. There are 18 pasta dishes, our favorite being the stuffed homemade manicotti. The veal is top quality

and offered in a number of styles from piccante (in a lemony sauce) to rolletini (stuffed with prosciutto and cheese). For dessert, try the homemade cannoli. The restaurant has changed little in looks, either, over the years. Tables are set in partitioned alcoves and there are murals of Naples on the walls. Entrées and pizza (all à la carte) are priced from $4 to $6.50.

TOMMASO'S NEAPOLITAN RESTAURANT, 1042 Kearny Street, San Francisco. Telephone: (415) 398-9696. Hours: 5-11, Wednesday-Saturday; 4-10, Sunday. Cards: BA, MC. Reservations not accepted. Wine and beer only. Parking in nearby garage.

PASTA and SPAGHETTI

Spaghetti Marinara Sauce	4.00
Spaghetti with Meat Sauce	4.50
Spaghetti Meat Balls	4.25
Spaghetti with Meat Sauce and Mushrooms	4.75
Half Spaghetti and Half Ravioli	4.00
Half Spaghetti, Half Ravioli with Meat Balls or Sausage	4.50
Stuffed Manicotti (Homemade)	4.75
Stuffed Manicotti with Meat Balls or Sausage	5.50
Ravioli, Homemade	4.00
Ravioli with Meat Balls or Sausage	4.50
Spaghetti with Sausage	4.25
Spaghetti with Butter	4.00
Spaghetti with Olive Oil, Garlic and Parsley	4.75
Linguine with Clams — Red or White Sauce	4.75
Spaghetti with Calamari (Baby Squid) in Marinara Sauce	5.50
Spaghetti with Shrimp in Marinara Sauce	6.00
Spaghetti with Fresh Broccoli, Sauté Olive Oil and Garlic	4.75
Macaroni with Mushrooms, Olive Oil, Garlic, Parsley & Sausage	5.50

TOMMASO'S OVEN-BAKED SPECIALTIES and ENTREES

Veal Scaloppine Marsala (Imported Italian Wine)	5.50	Veal Scaloppine Parmigiana (With Melted Cheese)	5.50
Veal Scaloppine Fiorentina (Coated with Egg Yolk)	5.50	Chicken Cacciatore	6.00
Baked Egg Plant Parmigiana	4.75	Chicken, Marsala (Imported Italian Wine)	6.00
Veal Scaloppine Piccante (Lemon base)	5.50		
Veal with Fresh Peppers and Mushrooms (Sauté in Marinara Sauce)	5.50	Stuffed Veal Rolletini (Broiled, stuffed with Prosciutto Ham and Cheese)	6.00

TRADER VIC'S
International $$$

This branch of Trader Vic's is distinguished from all other links in this far-flung restaurant chain: It is the headquarters of Trader Vic Bergeron himself and is managed by his son, Lynn. In the sea of Polynesian artifacts, fishnets and carved tikis that characterize this and other Trader Vic outposts, there is an island of civilized decorum—the clublike Captain's Cabin, one of the city's most favored meeting places for socially prominent residents and celebrated visitors. It's difficult to get a reservation in the Cabin, but well worth the try. Navigating the seven seas of Vic's international menu can be confusing; we usually trust the recommendations of the captain. You won't go wrong, however, with the Indonesian rack of lamb, the butterfly steak or fresh salmon in season. And you're better off avoiding the Cantonese dishes; you'll fare better in Chinatown. The wine list features an extensive selection of California labels. Everything is à la carte and the tab can soar easily. But especially in the inner sanctum of the Captain's Cabin, we feel the experience is worth the price.

TRADER VIC'S, 20 Cosmo Place, San Francisco. Telephone: (415) 776-2232. Lunch: 11:30-2:30, Monday-Friday. Dinner: 5-12, daily; closed Thanksgiving and Christmas. Cards: AE, BA, CB, MC. Reservations required. Full bar service. Valet parking.

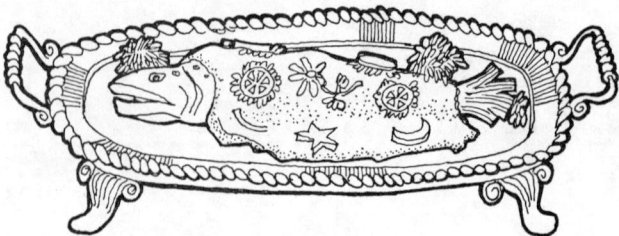

Trader Vic's Specialties

NEW YORK STEAK, MALAGASY... 12.00
Pepper steaks have been cooked
in conventional manner since
God knows when ... Try mine!

PAPER-THIN FILET OF BEEF 12.00
with Flaming Mustard Sauce

MINUTE STEAK MURAT 11.00

FILET TIPS BROCHETTE 9.00

MARROW BONE STEAK 12.00
with French Fried Onions

CALVES' SWEETBREADS 7.95
Trader Vic

GRILLED CALVES' SWEETBREADS . 7.95
On Canadian Bacon with Caper Sauce

MIXED GRILL CALCUTTA STYLE . 7.95

CHICKEN LIVERS SAUTÉ 6.50

CHICKEN LIVERS FLAMBÉ 7.75

KIDNEY SAUTÉ 6.50

MALAY PEANUT CHICKEN 6.50

VEAL PORT AU PRINCE
on Bed of Paké Noodles 8.75

CHOPPED SIRLOIN, MALAGASY.   7.00

KIDNEYS MARTINIQUE FLAMBÉ .. 7.75
with Sour Cream

FROGS LEGS SAUTÉ* 7.75
Trader Vic Style

BUTTERFLY STEAK 12.00
Hong Kong Style

CHICKEN STROGANOFF 6.50

LEMON BUTTER VEAL 8.25

CHOPPED NEW YORK STEAK 7.50
Hawaiian

VEAL WITH MOREL MUSHROOM .. 8.75

PORK CHOPS FORT SUTTER...... 6.75

CHICKEN SAUTÉ 6.75
Trader Vic Style

PYRAMID OF BEEF COSMO 12.00

BREAST OF CHICKEN
CORDON BLUE 6.50

Fish from the Lakes, Rivers and the Sea

MAHI MAHI FROM THE PACIFIC .. 5.25

MAHI MAHI SESAME 5.25

LOBSTER MOUSSE 8.50

BAKED STUFFED LOBSTER
THERMIDOR 12.50

BROILED LOBSTER 12.50
with Caper Sauce

DEVILED CRAB 8.50

PAKÉ CRAB* 9.50
HALF PORTION 5.00

ABALONE, MONTEREY STYLE 9.50

FILET OF SOLE, HELEN CAMERON . 7.75
Poached Sole — Olympia Oysters in Sauce
Mariniere.

FILET OF REX SOLE MEUNIÈRE .. 5.75

REX SOLE, FLORENTINE 6.85
with Cheese Sauce

REX SOLE TRADER VIC 7.75
with Crab Legs

FILET OF BUTTERFISH MURAT ... 6.85
Pan Broiled

BAY SCALLOPS MEUNIÈRE 7.25

FILET OF REX SOLE............. 7.00
with California Shrimps

ICELANDIC SCAMPI
SAN FRANCISCO STYLE 9.50
Delicately Seasoned Scampi Sauté with a
Light Creamed Wine Sauce — Covered
with Crisp Croutons, Shredded Parmesan
Cheese. Served with Steamed
Rice.

POACHED SALMON* 9.50
with Red Caviar Sauce

BARBECUED SALMON* 8.25

OYSTERS, ENGLISH STYLE 5.75
... skewered with bacon and mushrooms,
grilled and served with Hot Lemon Butter

BLUE POINT OYSTERS
ON THE HALF SHELL 3.95

OYSTERS FLORENTINE 5.75
...covered with chopped spinach leaves,
topped with Sauce Mornay, grated Parmesan cheese and baked

OYSTERS, HAMBOURG STYLE 5.75
...dipped in grated Parmesan cheese,
beaten egg, and then fine bread crumbs ...
fried in butter

CURRIED OYSTERS 6.50
...poached in white wine and removed ...
curry sauce. Served with steamed rice

OYSTER SAN JUAN
ON HALF SHELL 6.95
Deviled Crab on Top and Grilled

TRADER VIC'S SPECIAL OYSTER . 7.75
in Chafing Dish Flambé

95

San Francisco: Chinatown
TUNG FONG
Chinese Dim Sum $

One of the oldest dim sum restaurants in Chinatown, and still at its original capacity (which is small), Tung Fong is a well-kept secret and you'll see very few Caucasians here. Tray after tray comes out of the tiny kitchen with a seemingly endless variety of delicate morsels: chopped mushrooms in half-moons of rice dough, Chinese spinach and meatballs, deep-fried sweet potato, meat dumplings—your whole lavish lunch coming to around $3. There's a take-out counter behind which you can see a small army of Chinese women skillfully folding, stuffing and steaming the dim sum.

TUNG FONG, 808 Pacific Avenue, San Francisco. Telephone: (415) 362-7115. Hours: 10-3; closed Monday. No cards. Parking in city lot at Vallejo and Powell. No alcoholic beverages.

San Francisco: Mission District
VENETIAN GLASS NEPHEW
American (Southern)

$

If you're homesick for down-home cooking, the remedy is here. Eating at the Nephew is like being invited for dinner at Aunt Pittypat's home in Atlanta. "And frankly, you'll have the same luck here as going to someone's house for dinner," admits Robert J. Johnson, owner and chef du "cuisine maison-Dixon." "Sometimes it's up, sometimes it's down." But it's all very Southern and very homelike. The storefront restaurant is furnished with Victorian artifacts, big oak tables, a mishmash of unmatched chairs and a grand piano which is often played by one of Johnson's friends. The menu varies according to Johnson's whim and sometimes there is a choice of entrée, sometimes not. Dinners ($5 to $6.50) start with a hearty soup like okra gumbo and a hefty salad. The night's special might be southern fried chicken, roast ham, Brunswick stew or baked pork chops served with vegetables the likes of black-eyed peas or greens. There are homemade biscuits or corn bread and luscious desserts, often pecan pie. Guests are asked to arrive between 6:30 and 8 for a single seating and often if it's crowded, parties of two will be seated together at larger tables. On many evenings Johnson and his singer and musician friends stage impromptu entertainment after dinner. On Sundays the Nephew serves a hearty brunch for $4.50 which starts with a champagne cocktail, the morning paper and fresh fruit compote. Then, a large plate of creamy quiche, bacon or sausage or pork chops, grits with country gravy and those homemade biscuits.

VENETIAN GLASS NEPHEW, 2698 Folsom Street, San Francisco. Telephone: (415) 826-2172. Dinner: from 6:30, Wednesday-Saturday; Sunday brunch: 11:30-2. No cards. Reservations advised. Wine only. Street parking.

San Francisco:
North Beach and Financial District
YANK SING
Chinese Dim Sum $

Yank Sing is one of the city's oldest dim sum parlors. The original locale near the Broadway tunnel always looked a little dreary, but a newer branch downtown has lots of charm—a light-splashed, airy room with a high skylight and brick walls hung with colorful banners. In both locations, though, you can eat your way to Nirvana as the seemingly endless procession of trays appear, laden with the flavorful steamed or deep-fried dumplings containing a myriad of chopped meats and vegetables and ranging in flavor from savory to sweet. After you have eaten all you can, you are charged by the number of empty plates on the table—75 cents per plate.

YANK SING, 53 Stevenson (between First and Second) and 671 Broadway, San Francisco. Telephones: Stevenson, (415) 495-4510; Broadway, (415) 781-1111. Stevenson hours: 11 am-3 pm, Monday-Friday. Broadway hours: 10-5 daily. No cards. No reservations. Wine only. Parking difficult at both locales.

Marin County

Mill Valley
DAVOOD'S
Middle Eastern   **$$**

Rough-hewn redwood walls rise upward to a high skylight which is open on balmy days. Plants cascade from the ceiling and mosaics of stained glass are set here and there. In this spectacular setting you can enjoy anything from a casual snack to a full dinner, featuring the Persian specialties of owner Davood Kohanzadeh's family. Dinners ($6 to $12) include a salad or an exotic soup such as white bean with eggplant, cold cucumber and yoghurt, or the Persian aash. Baskets of freshly baked honey breads and rolls are on the table. For entrées you can choose from a selection of mild curries (seafood, vegetable, chicken, lamb); chicken, lamb or beef kebabs; unusual casseroles; trout or poached salmon with hollandaise. Plates come beautifully garnished with sautéed vegetables, turmeric rice and fresh fruit. The dolma appetizers (grape leaves stuffed with lamb and dried fruits) are among the best we have tasted. And the home-made pastries are truly sumptuous—walnut pie, cheesecake, baklava. At lunch Davood's offers salads, open-faced sandwiches, a cheese board and much more.

DAVOOD'S, 22 Miller, Mill Valley. Telephone: (415) 388-2000. Hours: 11 am-10 pm, daily. Cards: AE, BA, MC. Wine only. Parking in city lot across the street.

Mill Valley
DON PANCHO'S
Mexican   **$**

Don Pancho is Pancho Villa and this small hacienda is a veritable picture gallery of his exploits. Walls are hung with photographs of Pancho as a youth, Pancho and his women, Pancho and his guns. Sydney Gabriel, owner of this restaurant, is obviously a Pancho aficionado; his first venture was the popular Pancho Villa's in New York. In 1976 he transformed an old house in Mill Valley into a Mexican casa with whitewash and tiles. Among highlights of the menu are a delicious chicken mole and an unusual mole verde, a mild green sauce made from pumpkin seeds. There is a traditional arroz con pollo and a spicy chicken Mexicana with tomatoes and onions. Ceviche and sopapillas appear among the side dishes. There's a rich Mexican chocolate, with cinnamon and cream; coffee is from Oaxaca. Prices range from $3.95 for huevos rancheros to $7.50 for steak.

DON PANCHO'S, 24 Sunnyside Avenue, Mill Valley. Telephone: (415) 388-9868. Hours: 4-10, Monday-Thursday; 4-11, Friday-Sunday. No cards. Reservations not accepted. Wine and beer only. Easy parking.

Sausalito
GUERNICA
French/Basque $$

This whitewashed cottage, with its bed of hollyhocks and leaded-glass windows, looks as if it belongs in the European countryside rather than the outskirts of Sausalito. The interior retains the country-inn atmosphere with the window tables separated by panels of stained glass. To the left, there is a cozy bar where a classical guitarist plays on weekends. The cooking of owner Roger Minhondo reflects both his Basque heritage and his Parisian apprenticeship. Dinners ($6.50 to $8.50) include salad or soup; we'd opt for the latter, especially the hearty cheese-crusted French onion. When the fish are available fresh, Roger concocts one of the Bay Area's best bouillabaisses, served with French bread and a bowlful of aioli sauce to impart more garlic to the stew. The duckling with green olives is a favorite as are the homemade quenelles. Desserts, à la carte, include an excellent chocolate mousse and an unusual crème vanille.

GUERNICA, 2009 Bridgeway, Sausalito. Telephone: (415) 332-1512. Hours: 5-10:30; until 11, Friday and Saturday. Cards: AE, BA, MC. Reservations advised. Wine only.

San Rafael
LA MARMITE
French

$$

Yves Larguinat, former sous-chef at Ernie's, and Franz Prossegger, formerly of Paris, opened this charming restaurant in 1974. Candlelit tables are set with sparkling glasses, white napery and flowers. The service is friendly and professional. Dinner prices include a delicious soup—perhaps watercress or cream of vegetable—and a salad of butter lettuce with sliced mushrooms and hearts of palm. The entrées are beautifully garnished and served at the table with fresh vegetables, selected especially to accompany the main dish—not the same vegetable for everyone. À la carte appetizers, soups, salads and desserts are also available. Altogether, a very pleasant dining experience awaits you.

LA MARMITE, 909 Lincoln Avenue, San Rafael. Telephone: (415) 456-4020. Hours: 6-10:30; closed Monday. Cards: BA, MC. Reservations advised. Wine and beer only. Parking in nearby lot.

 # LE DINER

Le Potage du Jour

❁

La Salade Maison

❁

Cuisses de Grenouilles Provençale 7.75
Frog Legs Sauté, Garlic, Mushrooms, Tomatoes

Quenelles Normande 7.75
Quenelles, Shrimp

Suprême de Saumon Poché Hollandaise 7.50
Poached Salmon, Hollandaise Sauce

Filets de Sole Meunière ou Amandine . . . 6.50
Filets of Sole, Butter, Lemon or Butter, Almonds

Coq au Vin Vieux 7.00
Chicken in Burgundy Sauce

Le Canard Rôti à l'Orange (2) 16.50
Roast Duck, Flamed, Sauce Bigarade

Médaillons de Veau Dijonnaise 7.75
Medallions of Veal, Mustard Sauce

Ris-de-Veau en Ecrin 7.50
Braised Sweetbreads, Madeira Sauce

Lapin Sauté, Martini 7.75
Rabbit Sauté, Vermouth Sauce

Emincée de Boeuf aux Champignons . . . 7.25
Filet of Beef, Sliced Mushrooms, Madeira Sauce

Steak au Poivre 8.75
Pepper Steak, Green Pepper Corns, Flamed

Tournedos Béarnaise 8.75
Filet of Beef Broiled, Béarnaise Sauce

Filet de Boeuf en Croûte 9.25
Filet of Beef in Pastry Shell

Carré d'Agneau Provençale (2) 18.50
Roast Rack of Lamb

❁

Café

San Anselmo
LORENZO'S
Italian $$

Expatriot New Yorkers have transplanted here that style of Italian restaurant that is distinctively "New York." Fresh clams and mussels are flown in from the East Coast, as is a special Italian sausage, and even the imported Italian pasta is brought in from New York, for lack of a local source. The chef is a wizard of sauces and anything "marinara" will be delectably redolent with herbs. The veal is white and tender and ranges in presentation from a classic piccata with lemon, butter and capers to a most unusual saltimbocca, baked on a bed of spinach with prosciutto and mozzarella. Other rarely encountered dishes include an appetizer of deep-fried mozzarella slices, sauced with marinara, and a pasta of mostaccioli with chopped broccoli in a creamy cheese sauce. Among the desserts is a first-rate cannoli and a pretty pink "zambione," a blend of frothy eggs whipped with strawberries. The setting is as enjoyable as the food. The small wood-paneled dining room is intimate, candlelit, romantic. The service is excellent. The wine list contains a choice selection from small California vintners. We rate Lorenzo's as Marin County's best Italian restaurant and one of the finest in Northern California.

LORENZO'S, 729 Sir Francis Drake Boulevard, San Anselmo. Telephone: (415) 453-2552. Hours: 5-11, Tuesday-Saturday; 4-10, Sunday. Sunday brunch: 10-2. Cards: AE, BA, MC. Wine and beer only. Reservations advised. Complimentary valet parking. Private dining room for parties of eight.

Appetizers

Mozzarella Marinara	1 75
Baked Clams	3 50
Cold Antipasto	2 75
Shrimp Scampi or Marinara	4 00
Homemade Manicotti	2 50

Zuppa

Minestrone	1 00
Zuppa di Giorno	1 00

Pasta

Homemade Stuffed Shells	4 75
Homemade Manicotti	4 75
Homemade Ravioli	4 75
Mostacioli w/Broccoli	4 50
Linguini w/Fresh Clams	5 50
Linguini Carbonara	4 50
Le Fettuccine ~ Blanc or Verde	4 50

~ Above dishes served w/ Mixed Green Salad ~

Entrees

Shrimp Marinara or FraDiavolo	7 50
Catch of the Day	
Lobster Tails ~ Cooked to Order	10 00

Veal Milanese	7 00
Veal Scallopine alla Marsala	7 75
Veal Scallopine Francese	7 75
Veal Piccata	7 75
Veal Rollatine	8 25
Saltimbocca alla Romana	8 25

Chicken Parmigiana	6 00
Chicken Francese	6 00
Chicken Rollatine w/ Mushrooms	7 00

Above served w/ Mixed Green Salad & Fresh Vegetable of the Day

Specialties

Veal Parmigiana w/ Baked Ziti	6 50
Eggplant Parmigiana w/ Spaghetti	5 30

Inverness
MANKA'S
Czech/Viennese

$$

Manka's is everyone's dream of what a country inn should be. In an old house in a hilly, woodsy setting just beyond the tiny village of Inverness, owners Milan and Judy Prokupek provide some of the best central European cooking in the state. Dinners include a visit to an hors d'oeuvre table laden with Norwegian and Dutch herring, Danish and Norwegian cheeses, sausages, salamis, cold meats, fresh fruit, salads, relishes and flat breads. Then comes a homemade soup, perhaps caraway seed, asparagus, potato, lentil or cauliflower. The entrées are rich, subtly seasoned and accompanied by fresh vegetables. But no matter how satisfied you are at this point, don't miss the lavish cart of homemade Czech pastries. If the long drive back to San Francisco worries you, stay overnight. The inn has four bedrooms and five cottages which may be rented for $16.50 the night. A full breakfast in the Czech style is served.

MANKA'S CZECH RESTAURANT, Callender Way and Argyle, Inverness. Telephone: (415) 669-1034. Hours: 8:30 am-11 am, 6-8:30; Sunday dinner, 4:30-8; closed Tuesday and Wednesday; also closed Monday and Thursday in wintertime. Cards: AE, MC. Reservations required. Wine and beer only.

Entrees

Vepřová Pečeně
(ROAST PORK A LA CZECH) $7.95

Pečená Kachna
(ROAST DUCKLING WITH A LIGHT CARAWAY SAUCE) $8.25

Telecí Řízky na Houbách a Víně
(VEAL SLICES WITH MUSHROOMS AND WINE) $8.75

Telecí Maso na Paprice
(CUBES OF VEAL IN A SUBTLE PAPRIKA SAUCE) $8.25

Telecí Řízky Smažené
(BREADED VEAL SLICES, VIENNESE STYLE) $7.50

Smažené Kuře
(BREADED CHICKEN, VIENNESE STYLE) $7.25

Ustřice Z Tomales Bay Pečené na Sardelovém Masle
(OYSTERS BAKED ON THE HALF SHELL WITH ANCHOVY BUTTER) $8.25

Hovězi Guláš
(CUBES OF BEEF IN A RICH, HEARTY SAUCE) $7.95

Beverages

COFFEE   SANKA   TEA   MILK

Desserts

MANKA'S CZECH PASTRIES (From the Cart) $1.25

PRICE OF ENTREE INCLUDES HORS D' OEUVRES,
SOUP, ENTREE, VEGETABLES, ROLLS AND COFFEE.

San Rafael
MAURICE ET CHARLES BISTROT
French $$$

From the street it looks like a corner saloon. Inside is pure bistrot with a long, old-fashioned bar and friendly graffiti on the walls. In the kitchen is Claude Collomb, a chef of enormous talent, trained in the gastronomic capitol of Lyons. Actually, the Bistrot would be more accurately named Maurice et Claude, for he is co-owner with Maurice Amzallag, former La Bourgogne maître d'. (That should tell you something about the service.) And the Bistrot is now *sans* Charles, a.k.a. founding partner Robert Charles, who has relocated at Lake Tahoe. But it is Claude's cooking which makes this place extraordinary. The menu changes periodically, in keeping with the season. Usually present though are the quenelles, a triumph of feather-light fish dumplings bathed in a sauce of lobster and truffles. (An order may be split as an appetizer.) Another perennial favorite is the saddle of lamb, which is sometimes served in a light pastry shell, à la Wellington, sometimes stuffed with sorrel. The salade St. Raphael is sensational. One word of warning though: Bring cash and a heap of it. Prices are à la carte, wines are expensive, only American Express cards are accepted, and personal checks are adamantly refused.

MAURICE ET CHARLES BISTROT, 901 Lincoln Avenue, San Rafael. Telephone: (415) 456-2010. Hours: 6:30-10:30, Monday-Saturday. Cards: AE. Reservations required. Wine and beer only. Public parking in rear of building.

SPÉCIALITÉS

Quenelles Truffées du Bistrot   7.50
Fish delicacy with sliced mushrooms, lobster sauce

Suprêmes de Volaille a l'Orange   8.00
Tender breasts of chicken, orange sauce

Médaillons de Veau Sautés a l'Oseille   10.00
White veal with sorrel, sauce au champagne

Aiguillettes de Canard Sautées aux Pommes   9.00
Breasts of duckling, sauce with Porto wine, apples

Croustade d'Agneau aux deux Purées (for two)   20.00
Young lamb saddle in pastry shell, sauce menthe

Cassoulet Toulousain   10.00
Southern France famous lamb stew

Saumon Frais   §   Marcassin   (en saison)
Fresh salmon   *Young wild boar*

Sausalito
SEVEN SEAS
Seafood $

On weekends it seems that half the town of Sausalito is in Seven Seas' crowded bar, swapping sailing stories and local gossip with owner Paul DeMoss. In the rear are two garden rooms, perfect for outdoor dining in balmy weather. Fresh seafood is the attraction here—a nearly perfect bouillabaisse, poached or grilled salmon or halibut, calamari, steamed cherrystone clams, a selection of seafood casseroles and more. Portions are bountiful and entrées are priced around $5, with a salad included with some. A lot of food for the price.

SEVEN SEAS, 682 Bridgeway, Sausalito. Telephone: (415) 332-1304. Hours: 11:30-11:30, Sunday-Thursday; 11:30-12:30, Friday and Saturday. Cards: AE, BA, DC, MC. Reservations advised. Full bar service. Street parking or in city lots.

Sausalito
SOUPÇON
American/Continental $$

Soupçon figuratively means a "slight taste, a dash." That's a misnomer here. While this may well qualify as the world's smallest restaurant, seating only about 20, there's more than a "slight taste" in the generous amounts of food. In their tiny kitchen proprietors Ford and Jackie Cook brew up two kettles of heavenly soups daily and give them funny names like Shirley Katz or Old Sid Foster's Mountain Dew. The contents are equally intriguing—Jamaican black beans with rum and bananas, spinach and oysters, old-fashioned New England seafood chowder, to name only a few. There are also sandwiches as high as your hand, gorgeous salads served with homemade nut bread, and the richest of desserts. You can lunch here for only $1.50 or go for the full dinner ($5.25 to $7.35), which includes some of that wonderful soup, plus salad and garlic or herb bread. Entrées change nightly but there is usually a choice of fresh fish and steak Dijon, cooked with mustard and Swiss cheese. Prawns Malabar are a recurring favorite, as is the "Katherine Fletcher," a breast of chicken with avocado and cheese. Soupçon offers a good selection of California wines at very reasonable prices.

SOUPÇON, 49 Caledonia Street, Sausalito. Telephone: (415) 332-9752. Hours: 11:30-2:45, 6-10, Monday-Saturday; noon-8, Sunday. No cards. Reservations advised. Wine only. Street parking.

Ross
SWISS CELLAR
Swiss $$

Behind a storefront facade on the Ross Commons is a romantic little hideaway serving exquisite food at reasonable prices with we-really-care service. There is a warm glow of candlelight against brick and wood walls, hanging plants, fresh flowers on immaculately set tables, a relaxed ambience of well-being. Though owner Roger Braun and his wife Marianne are German Swiss, the restaurant's menu reflects the ethnic heterogeneity of his native land, with emphasis on French cooking and a smattering of Italian and Germanic dishes. Roger often does typical Swiss recipes as nightly specials. Dinners include a delicious salad of butter lettuce, plum tomatoes and artichoke hearts. The veal and the chicken dishes are of high quality and the rack of lamb is excellent, too. Of the à la carte extras here, we would bypass the snails, served sans shells, but opt for the mocha parfait, made with rich, refreshing homemade coffee ice cream.

SWISS CELLAR, 9 Ross Commons, Ross. Telephone: (415) 461-5566. Hours: 11:30-2:30, 6-10, Tuesday-Friday; 5:30-10, Saturday and Sunday. Cards: BA, MC. Reservations essential. Wine and beer only. Street parking.

San Rafael
YOSHIDA
Japanese $

A surprisingly broad selection of beautifully prepared dishes in bountiful portions is to be found at this unpretentious little restaurant. Dinners, priced from $4.10 to $4.60, include a cucumber-carrot salad and soup. Seafood is emphasized in Yoshida's entrées. There is a feather-light prawns tempura, deep-fried oysters, yosenabe (a sort of Japanese bouillabaisse), and sliced salmon, mackerel or squid, basted with teriyaki sauce. One-pot (nabemono) dishes include sukiyaki, shabu shabu and chicken mizutaki. There are also chicken and beef teriyakis, yakitori and gyoza, pan-fried pork and vegetables folded into a won ton skin. Sushi, donburi and sashimi, too. You won't go away either hungry or impoverished from here.

YOSHIDA, 810 Third Street, San Rafael. Telephone: (415) 456-3844. Hours: 11:45-2, 5-9:30, Tuesday-Friday; 5-9:30, Saturday. No cards. Reservations not necessary. Beer and sake only. Parking lot.

East Bay

Berkeley
À LA CARTE
French

$$

The dining room is petite and plain, with only about eight wood-topped tables (some in booths), a corner fireplace and a partial view of the kitchen. But the cooking is truly grand. Owner John Zuska prepares only two entrées each night from a large and creative repertoire. Fresh baby trout, weighing in at four ounces, appears on his menu frequently in various guises—stuffed with either salmon mousse, mushrooms, spinach, or sorrel, or even wrapped in lettuce leaves. Other dishes might be classically simple, like a roast filet of beef served with fresh peas in artichoke-bottom cups. A soup and salad choice also changes nightly and bears witness to Zuska's imaginative culinary flair. Frog legs soup? He does this, as well as purée of chestnut, cream of artichoke, veloutés of mushroom or sorrel. Salads might be a heavenly remoulade of celeriac bursting with herbs, sliced mushrooms, or a combination of beans, bacon and cauliflower. And don't overlook the desserts: perhaps strawberries topped with a Marsala sabayon or a tart homemade ice of fresh pears. Periodically Zuska prepares special dinners from various regions of France. Prices, as the name implies, are à la carte. A three-course dinner will average about $9 per person.

À LA CARTE, 1453 Dwight Way, Berkeley. Telephone: (415) 548-2322. Hours: 6-9:30, Tuesday-Saturday. No cards. Reservations required. Street parking.

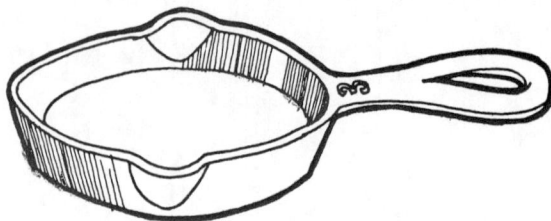

Oakland
CHEZ JOSEPH
French/Canadian

$$

This century-old house on the Bret Harte Boardwalk was built by an early mayor of Oakland and it exudes Victorian charm—high ceilings, marble fireplaces, brocade-covered tables, a gilt-framed mirror about 12 feet high. Joseph, who started the restaurant, has since gone on to new ventures, and it is now the house of Jerry Jessop, a chef of long experience, and his Canadian wife, Pat. Into a rather standard collection of French entrées, the Jessops have introduced a few dishes inspired by the foods of Pat's homeland. In tribute to French Quebec there is pork cordon bleu, a chop stuffed with Canadian bacon and Swiss cheese. Honoring Ontario is roast pheasant, sauced with sour cream and mushrooms, garnished with fresh fruit. Nova Scotia is given credit for a rolled filet of sole, stuffed with shrimp and crab, and bathed with a sauce velouté. Dinners ($6.25 to $12) include a choice of soup or a small plate of pasta covered with a garlicky sauce of minced clams. Then comes a salad (organically grown romaine lettuce from Salinas, when available) with Jerry's fantastic creamy tarragon dressing. For dessert, try the "leopard," a refreshing parfait of orange juice and currant jelly. Mrs. Jessop is the hostess and her graciousness and attentiveness to her guests' needs make dining here a very special experience.

CHEZ JOSEPH, 567 Fifth Street, Oakland. Telephone: (415) 444-6183. Lunch: 11:30-2, Tuesday-Friday. Dinner: 6-10, Tuesday-Saturday. Cards: BA, MC. Reservations advised. Wine only. Street parking.

Berkeley
IL PAVONE
Northern Italian

$$

The concept of the menu here is as intellectual as the chef. Morris Kau was born in Hong Kong, received a master's in philosophy from the University of Rochester, studied provincial cooking in France and was chef at Narsai's before he and partner Paul Marner opened Il Pavone. Despite his Chinese background and French culinary training, he chose to feature the more esoteric dishes of northern Italy in his own restaurant because he did not want to compete with Narsai's and other fine French restaurants in Berkeley, and because the influence of surrounding countries—Hungary and particularly France—on northern Italian cuisine fascinated him. Thus you find here dishes rarely encountered elsewhere—squid stuffed with spicy minced mushrooms, a curried coquille St. Jacques, pasta with scallops—all little-known regional specialties of Italy. His nightly specials often run to the esoteric (rolled filet of beef stuffed with whole quail eggs). Kau also enjoys preparing dishes not on the menu as requested by customers. Consult him in advance for a special party. He is a purist, too, insisting on fresh vegetables and refusing to serve veal because white veal is virtually unobtainable within his budget (dinners are priced under $10). You enter Il Pavone through a brick-paved courtyard into a pleasant wide-windowed bar. The dining room is informal with wood-topped tables, white-washed brick walls and rather incongruous ruffled shades on hanging lamps.

IL PAVONE, 1730 Shattuck Avenue, Berkeley. Telephone: (415) 548-0400. Hours: 6-9, Tuesday-Sunday. Cards: BA, MC. Reservations advised. Full bar service.

· Insalata ·

Insalata Della Casa	house salad	1 25
Melanzane Marinate	marinated eggplant	1 95
Funghi sott'Olio	mushrooms in herbed vinegar and oil	1 95

· Antipasti ·

Galamari Ripeni Con Funghi · baked squid stuffed with mushrooms		2 75
Crostata Di Porro · baked pastry of cheeses, eggs, bacon and leeks		2 00
Antipasto Misto ·		2 25
Minestra Del Giorno · house soup of the day		1 50

· Paste ·

Linguine All'Acciugato · with anchovy, garlic and oil		5 85
Linguine Con Conchiglie Saint-Jacques · with scallops		7 75
Tagliatelle Alla Garibaldina · with tomato, cheese and cream		6 75
Tagliatelle Con Salsicce · with sausage		7 75
Tagliatelle Alla Bolognese · with a rich herbed tomato sauce		5 85

· Dolce ·

Gelato Alla Maurizio · our own ice cream		1 25
Spuma Alla Pavone · A Rich Mousse		1 00
Pasticceria · pastry of the day		1 75

Cena Completa Incluso Minestra e Insalata

Galamari Ripeni Con Funghi · baked squid stuffed with mushrooms		7 25
Conchiglie Saint-Jacques Con Curry · bay scallops with curry		8 50
Animelle Con Pepe Verde · Sauteed sweetbreads with green peppercorns		8 25
Salsicce Alla Bolognese · Sausage in a rich tomato sauce		8 25
Medaglione Di Filetto · Sauteed fillet of beef with a rich veal sauce		9 75

· Sales Tax will be added to the price of all food and Beverage ·

Due to water conservation please ask if you desire a glass of water

117

Berkeley
LA PEÑA
Latin American

$

A *peña* is a Latin American social and cultural center where people can eat as well. Berkeley's La Peña was organized by a group of Latin-Americans to diffuse the culture and foods of their countries. Woven baskets and South American artifacts are hung on the walls of the spacious dining room, where large tables are covered with checkered cloths. A profusion of literature espouses a number of political and social causes. The food is virtually a culinary tour from Mexico to the tip of Argentina—at incredibly low prices. Less than $2.50 brings you sopa marinera, a sort of Chilean bouillabaisse of white fish and shellfish cooked with potatoes and vegetables; or a Caribbean concoction of eggplant baked with onions and red pimentos in coconut cream, served with black beans and fresh fruit. Prices soar up to $3.50 for milaneza, an Argentinian beef cutlet topped with tomatoes, avocados and melted cheese; or up to $4.50 for the big splurge of Mexican enchiladas containing crab, bay shrimp, cheese, tomatoes and onions. A delicious soup or a nondescript salad is included in the dinner price, plus freshly made corn chips and hot bread. You won't go away hungry or much poorer.

LA PEÑA CULTURAL CENTER AND RESTAURANT, 3105 Shattuck Avenue, Berkeley. Telephone: (415) 849-2568. Lunch: 11:30-2, Tuesday-Friday. Dinner: 6-10, Tuesday-Sunday. No cards. Wine and beer only.

Oakland
LOVE'S PAGAN'S DEN
Philippine

$$

Ben and Art Love have a penchant for opening restaurants in unlikely places. They started their Pagan's Den in a run-down neighborhood behind a massage parlor and then moved to a modernized Victorian with a sweeping view of the BART tracks and the railroad freight yards. But the Philippine food is truly delightful. Start with an à la carte order of lumpia—crisp, deep-fried pastry stuffed with a mixture of chicken, pork, shrimp and vegetables. Dinners ($3.95 to $6.95) include a tangy Philippine soup, a Caesar-type salad and a choice of entrées. These range from sauté dishes (crab in black bean sauce, sweet and sour pork, chicken adobo in garlic-vinegar sauce) to pancit (noodle dishes) to rellenong manok, the traditional festival dish of the Philippines (roasted game hen stuffed with chorizo, pork and spices). There is also an exotic combination of lobster, coconut milk and ginger for $12.50. For dessert try the leche plan, a rich sweet custard.

LOVE'S PAGAN'S DEN, 760 East Eighth Street, Oakland. (From San Francisco, take the Jackson exit off the Nimitz (Freeway.) Telephone: (415) 832-3383. Hours: 11:30-2, 5-midnight, Tuesday-Friday; 5-midnight, Saturday. Cards: BA,MC. Reservations advised. Full bar service. Street parking.

Berkeley
NARSAI'S
Continental

$$$

Located in a residential section of the Berkeley hills, Narsai's offers a repertoire of classic French cooking interspersed with the Assyrian dishes of owner Narsai David's parents. The setting is contemporary chic: some walls paneled with redwood staves from an old Oakland reservoir, others painted stark white and hung with Oriental rugs, modern paintings and massive metal sculptures. Prices might seem high at first, but included in the dinner are five courses with a choice of soups (perhaps mushroom and clam, chilled watercress, or cold spinach potage) and hors d'oeuvre (herrings with apples and sour cream, dolmas, gnocchi baked in a tart shell, or quiche, to name a few of the changing selections. A light salad follows the entrée as a prelude to the superbly rich desserts, made by Narsai's own pastry chef. The wine list here is one of the best in the Bay Area with some 500 bottlings including such collectibles as a 1945 Chateau La Tour and a 1928 Haut Brion. The California list is vast, with almost all of the exciting small wineries represented. On Monday evenings Narsai's features a special five-course dinner from another country, ranging the western hemisphere from Scandinavia to Latin America. For the budget conscious or light eaters, three-course dinners are available between 5 and 6:30 nightly for $3 under the menu price. And if you don't feel like cooking on the holidays, Narsai's is good to know about: There is a festive, traditional dinner served on Thanksgiving, Christmas and New Year's Eve.

NARSAI'S, 385 Colusa Avenue, Berkeley. Telephone: (415) 527-7900. Hours: 5-10, Sunday-Thursday; 5-11, Friday and Saturday. Cards: AE, BA, CB, DC, MC. Reservations advised. Full bar service. Parking lot next door.

L'AUBERGINE A LA TURQUE 9.50
EGGPLANT, BAKED WITH A STUFFING OF LAMB,
SEASONED WITH TOMATOES, ONIONS AND BASIL.

LES GRENADINS DE BOEUF   10.50
A L'ESTRAGON
THIN SLICES OF FILET MIGNON SAUTEED
WITH FRESH MUSHROOMS AND TARRAGON,
AND FLAMBEED WITH RED WINE.

LE CONTRE-FILET EN CROUTE,
SHULAMITH 12.50
NEW YORK OF LAMB, SPREAD WITH MUSHROOM DUXELLE
AND WRAPPED IN A FLAKY CRUST THEN ROASTED
MEDIUM RARE AND SERVED WITH SAUCE BORDELAISE.

LE CARRE D'AGNEAU, ASSYRIEN   11.00
RACK OF LAMB, MARINATED IN POMEGRANATE
JUICE, RED WINE, ONIONS, AND BASIL,
THEN ROASTED TO YOUR ORDER.

LE FILET DE POISSON POCHE   10.50
EN VOL AU VENT
FRESH FILET OF FISH IN SEASON POACHED IN WHITE WINE
WITH SHRIMP; THEN SERVED IN A VOL AU VENT WITH A
SAUCE OF THE NATURAL JUICES REDUCED WITH CREAM.

LES QUENELLES
DE SAUMON, NANTUA 9.50
SALMON MOUSSE, POACHED LIGHTLY AND SERVED
WITH A RICH CREAMED VELOUTE
MADE WITH THE POACHING LIQUID.

LES CALMARS AU CRABE 9.50
SQUID, STUFFED WITH CREAMED CRAB MEAT,
AND BAKED WITH DRAWN BUTTER.

LES SUPREMES DE VOLAILLE,
ALEXIS BESPALOFF 9.50
THINLY SLICED MEDALLIONS OF CHICKEN BREAST,
SAUTEED IN BUTTER WITH FRESH CREAM AND FLAMBEED
WITH SAUTERNE TO CREATE A RICH, DELICATE SAUCE.

Hayward
OSCAR'S BISTRO
French

$$

Oscar is not the owner nor the chef. Oscar is the name of a stuffed pheasant perched by the door. The drab exterior of this cottage belies the romantic, flock-papered, candlelit ambience within. Owner Daniel Vien-Chevreux is a gracious host; his partner Donald Buhrz cooks, with a heavy hand on the herbs. The dinner price includes a green salad with a perky herb dressing, a dollop of tagliarini with clams in a piquant pepper sauce, the entrée, and cognac pudding for dessert. We once criticized Oscar's for serving snails sans shells, and as a result the à la carte escargots are now encased in ceramic shells. The entrées can be variable at times, but altogether Oscar's is by far the best restaurant we have found in the Hayward-San Leandro Area.

OSCAR'S BISTRO, 21181 Foothill Boulevard (Hayward exit off MacArthur Freeway), Hayward. Telephone: (415) 538-3522. Hours: 6-9:30, Tuesday-Thursday; 6-10:30, Friday and Saturday. Cards: BA, MC. Reservations advised. Wine only. Parking lot.

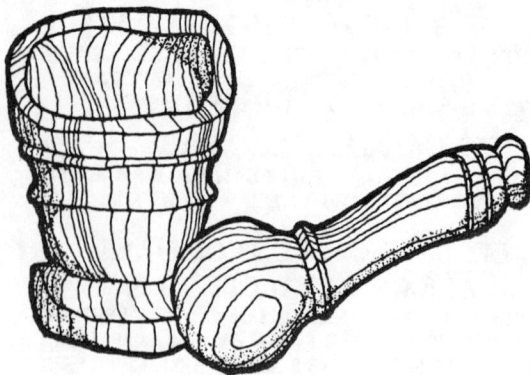

Tournedoes Sautees — 9.95
filet mignon - sauté mushrooms marsala.
sauce bearnaise

Filet en Brochette — 7.75
pieces of filet mignon, onions, bell
peppers and mushroom sauce.

Steak au Poivre — 9.75
New York pepper steak

Steak Diane — 9.95
New York steak, finished with cognac,
sherry and mushrooms.

Veaufarci `a la Florentine — 7.50
veal stuffed with finely chopped spinach
and cheese.

Veau Murat — 9.00
veal sauté, finished in cream sauce,
artichokes and mushrooms.

Suprême de Volaille Dijonnais — 7.00
breasts of chicken sautés, finished
with cream sauce, ham, and enriched
with dijon mustard.

Lobster Thermidor — 10.50
lobster sautéed in butter with
mushrooms and chives, blended
into a cream sauce and baked.

Lobster Tails — 9.50
lobster tails sautéed in butter.

Veal Oscar — 11.00
veal sautéed in butter, topped with
crab, asparagus, mushroom and
sauce bearnaise, "when available".

123

Oakland
ROARING CAMP CAFE
International $$

In one of the restored Victorians along Oakland's Bret
Harte Boardwalk, the Roaring Camp Mercantile Company
has opened a small cafe where the cooking is as fresh and
creative as the setting. The stark white walls are accented
with memorabilia—a turn-of-the-century Pepsi sign, plants
cascading from a medicine chest, a fern on a 12-foot-high
pedestal. Tables are covered with patchwork cloths over
quilted skirts, or laminated with blue checkered oilcloth. A
large redwood deck in the rear is open for al fresco lunch-
ing. Roaring Camp started out serving lunch and afternoon
snacks only, but now serves dinner as well, two nights a
month. Soups are unusual vegetable combinations, like a
cream of spinach and mushroom, served in a soufflé dish
with a puff-pastry cheese stick. At lunch, there are crêpes,
egg dishes, salads and some inventive open-faced sand-
wiches. Chutneyed chicken is a favorite: Slices of whole
wheat bread are topped with a lightly curried mixture of
chicken, celery chunks, raisins, grapes, nuts, scallions; chut-
ney is placed over this and all is baked with a light crown of
white cheese. Then there is the "mushroom madness": dark
rye bread smothered with marinated mushrooms and red
onions, topped with Swiss cheese and baked. For desserts
or snacks there are tea cakes made with fruits or nuts,
baked apples in puff pastry, or fruit crêpes. Prices of lunch
entrées average $3. Dinners are $10 and include appetizer,
soup, salad and choice of two entrées, dictated by the whim
of the chef.

ROARING CAMP CAFE, 571 Fifth Street, Oakland. Tele-
phone: (415) 451-0863. Hours: 11:30-2:30 for lunch;
2:30-4:30 for snacks; dinners served two Saturdays a
month by reservation. Closed Sunday. Cards: AE, BA, DC,
MC. Wine only. Parking under freeway off of Sixth Street.

Berkeley
TAIWAN RESTAURANT
Chinese

$

"We are proud to be the first restaurant in this country to serve Taiwan's version of China's epicurean delights," proclaims the menu of the Taiwan Restaurant. What is Taiwanese cuisine? It combines the cooking of the native population of the island and the dishes of those who have migrated from all over China—Manchuria, Hunan, Szechwan, Canton. The menu here is divided into traditional categories—appetizers, soups, seafood, fowl, etc.—with the addition of a category termed "Taiwanese specialties." From this section try the fish ball soup, delicately textured balls of ground fish in a clear peppery broth, or the Taiwan pickled cabbage with pork tripe in which thin strips of long-simmered tripe are combined with shredded cabbage, resulting in a slightly salty, perfectly textured dish. Other specialties of the island are three squid dishes, including a soup, and several pork dishes. Additional recommendations: General Tsuo's chicken, a Hunanese preparation of boneless chicken in a sauce dotted with chilis, a Mandarin braised bean curd with Chinese mushrooms, bamboo shoots and onions, a whole braised fish in brown bean sauce and several simple stir-fry vegetable dishes, spinach with garlic being especially good. Dinners will average about $5 per person. If you wish to try yet another facet of "Chinese" cuisine, the Taiwan offers an excellent opportunity.

TAIWAN RESTAURANT, 2071 University Avenue (corner of Shattuck), Berkeley. Telephone: (415) 845-1456. Hours: 11:30 am-9:30 pm, Monday, Tuesday, Thursday-Saturday; 4:30-9:30, Sunday. Cards: AE, BA, MC. Reservations advised for large parties. Wine and beer only.

Berkeley
WARSZAWA
Polish $$

The old house that this restaurant occupies is cozy, crowded, casual and filled with good aromas from the home cooking of the owners' native Warsaw. The menu is à la carte, but you rob yourself of some exceptional dishes if you don't eat your way through the menu. Don't miss the herring in sour cream, freshly made with slices of apples and onions added. The soups are excellent, too, especially the hot borsht, bursting with parsley, dill, carrots and onions, with a hard-cooked egg in the center. Of the entrées ($4.85 to $6.85) we especially like the pierogi, pelmeni-like pastry shells filled with meat, cheese and mushrooms, and cooked in butter. The crisp-skinned duckling is stuffed with apples and served with dumplings. Stuffed cabbage is filled with a spicy veal-beef-chicken mixture and topped with a paprika cream sauce. Other items include crêpes with meat and mushrooms, hunter's stew with beef, pork and sauerkraut, and beef roulade. Our favorite of the rich desserts is a walnut torte soaked with rum.

WARSZAWA, 1549 Shattuck Avenue, Berkeley. Telephone: (415) 841-5539. Hours: 5:30-10; closed Tuesday. No cards. Reservations advised. Beer and wine only. Street parking.

Peninsula

San Jose
EMILE'S SWISS AFFAIR
French/Swiss $$

Ask anyone to name San Jose's best restaurant and Emile's is the answer you are most likely to hear. The atmosphere is comfortable and quite European. The cooking is by owner/chef Emile Mooser who was trained in Lausanne. À la carte dinners here can be quite expensive, especially because it is difficult to resist the beguiling list of appetizers—fettucini Alfredo, quenelles Nantua, spinach salad, crayfish bisque, to name only a few. And it is almost a sin to decline Emile's masterful soufflé Grand Marnier. But for the budget conscious there is also a selection of dinners moderately priced from $6.50 to $11. With these you are served the soup of the day or a salad delicately sprinkled with chopped hard-cooked eggs, plus ice cream or sherbet. Entrée selections on the dinner include an unclassic piccata of veal, to which cream has been added; and le gschnatzlets Zurichoise, a Swiss dish of veal and pork in a delicate cream sauce.

EMILE'S SWISS AFFAIR, 545 South Second Street, San Jose. Telephone: (415) 289-1960. Hours: 5-10, Tuesday-Sunday. Cards: AE, BA, MC. Reservations advised. Wine and beer only. Parking lot.

Les Hors d'Oeuvre à la Carte

Les Crevettes sautées Bordelaise 3.75

Fettuccini Alfredo 2.50   Quenelles Nantua 3.25

Les Escargots de Bourgogne 3.75

Le Paté Maison, Garni 2.00   Salade Mimosa .90

Salade aux Epinards (fresh Spinach) 2.00

Potage du Jour .75   Bisque aux Ecrevisses 1.75

Soupe a l'Oignon, Gratinée 1.50

Nos Spécialités à la Carte

Les Noisettes d'Agneau, Parisienne 9.00
Lamb filet served with an herb-and-garlic butter

Le Tournedos, Bearnaise 9.50
Filet of Beef with sauce Bearnaise

L'Entrecôte au Poivre Vert de Madagascar 10.00
New York-cut peppersteak made with undried peppercorns

Les Crevettes sautées Bordelaise 9.50
Prawns sautéed with butter, garlic, and wine

Les Medaillons de Boeuf, Charcutiere 9.50
Beef filet with a sauce of butter, shallots, cream, mustard, cornichons

Les Fruits de Mer en Croustade 9.25
Selected seafoods in a lobster sauce served in a puff-pastry shell.

Les Ris de Veau, sauté Poulette 8.50
Veal Sweetbreads with a white wine sauce, finished with cream

Les Mignonettes de Veau aux Crevettes 10.00
White Veal combined with prawns-sautéed with lemon, butter, mushrooms

Les Grendines des Trois Rois 11.00
Filets of Beef, Veal, and Lamb, each with its own sauce

Les Escalopes de Veau, Vigneron 10.00
White Veal, sautéed with butter, shallots, wine, lemon, cream and seedless grapes

Palo Alto
LA TERRASSE
French/Belgian

$$

This comes close to being "that perfect little French restaurant" of which everyone dreams. There are three dining rooms with a country French feeling about them: floral-patterned wallpaper and drapes, white tablecloths, cane-backed chairs, candlelight. *Très romantique.* When weather permits, lunch and dinner are also served on an outside terrace. The owner is Belgian-trained chef Leon Sidella, founder and co-owner of San Francisco's La Maisonette and La Bergerie. Dinners here include soup and salad, but for a starter don't overlook the superb fondue de fromage Bruxelloise, a classic appetizer of Belgium. Three types of Swiss cheeses are blended with cream, egg yolks and nutmeg, then cut into squares, lightly breaded and deep fried so that a golden crust forms around the creamy cheese. Sidella's soups are usually cream-based and intricately seasoned, ranging from butter lettuce or watercress to tomato or lentil. The salad is a large mound of butter lettuce with a tart, creamy dressing. Of the entrées our favorite is filet of sole mouselet; small filets of sole encircling dollops of pale pink salmon mousse are poached and bathed with a sensational sauce of sorrel, white wine and cream. The wine list is not extensive, but is reasonably priced. Try the slightly effervescent Souverain Colombard. Lunches are priced from $4.25 to $6.95.

LA TERRASSE, 3740 El Camino Real, Palo Alto. Telephone: (415) 494-0700. Lunch: 11:30-2, Monday-Friday. Dinner: 5:30-10:30, Monday-Saturday. Cards: BA, MC. Full bar service. Reservations advised.

À la Carte

HORS D'OEUVRES

Escargots de Bourgogne	2.95
Crêpes de Fruits de Mer	2.75
Fondue de Fromage Bruxelloise	2.50
Paté Maison	2.50
Coeurs de Palmier	2.25

Le Dîner

(includes Soup & Salad)

ENTRÉES

Saumon Joinville — 7.75
poached salmon with brandy, cream & paprika

Coquille aux Fruits de Mer Normandie — 7.50
crab, shrimps & scallops on a seashell

Filet de Sole Mouselet — 7.25
with mousse of salmon

Poulet Sauté Mercédès — 6.75
chicken sautéed with mushrooms & chicken liver

Paupiette de Veau Champenoise — 7.50
rolled with ham & cheese

Gourmandise de Veau Deglasé au Citron — 7.50
veal sautéed in butter & lemon

Ris de Veau Financière — 7.50
sweetbreads in brandy, cream & mushrooms

Le Lapin Marchand de Vin — 7.75
rabbit marinated in wine & herbs

Le Canard Rôti au Grand Marnier — 8.00
roasted duck with orange sauce & grand marnier

Mignonnette de Filet Mathurini — 8.50
tenderloin beef with special sauce

Tournedos Massena — 9.50
filet mignon with madeira sauce

Le Carré d'Agneau "La Terrasse" (for 2) 19.00
rack of lamb with crust of garlic, shallots & butter

All food & beverages are subject to tax.
No personal checks — Minimum Charge 4.00

Menlo Park
LE POT AU FEU
French   **$$**

The dining room looks like a bustling Parisian sidewalk cafe, moved indoors. There is a raised platform in one corner, with tables, under large umbrellas, set with green and white plaid oilcloth covers and kerosene-burning lamps. Gleaming copperware hangs from the walls. Le Pot au Feu makes no pretense of elegance, but it is a cafe of exceptional charm and pizzazz. And the cooking of owner-chef Jean Cornil is excellent. Pot-au-feu, that standby of thrifty French housewives, is of course one of the specialties; the boiled brisket of beef is served with a mélange of fresh vegetables, hot mustard and gherkins. Another favorite is the Belgian rabbit in a light sauce of cream and mustard. Each night there is a different special. On Thursdays it's sweetbreads with mushrooms and cream sauce in a shell of

les Hors d'Oeuvre

Escargots de Bourgogne 3²⁵
Soupe à l'Oignon 1⁷⁵
Pâté du Chef 1⁷⁵
Salade Maison 1⁰⁰
Soupe du jour 1²⁵

le Spécial du Jour
(Includes soup, salad, french bread & butter)

* **Mardi** (Tuesday)   **Foie de Veau Persillade** 6⁵⁰
CALF LIVER SAUTEED IN BUTTER AND GARLIC - SPRINKLED WITH PARSLEY

* **Mercredi** (Wednesday)   **Coquilles St. Jacques** 7⁰⁰
SCALLOPS AND SEAFOOD IN A WHITE WINE CREAM SAUCE WITH MUSHROOMS

* **Jeudi** (Thursday)   **Feuilleté de Ris de Veau** 7⁰⁰
CALF SWEETBREADS IN A BASKET OF PUFF PASTRY, MUSHROOMS & CREAM SAUCE

* **Vendredi** (Friday)   **Gigot d'Agneau rôti aux herbes** 7⁵⁰
ROAST LEG OF LAMB IN ITS NATURAL JUICES, GARLIC & AROMATIC HERBS

* **Samedi** (Saturday)   **Filet de Boeuf en Croûte** 8⁵⁰
FILET MIGNON IN A CRUST, DUXELLE OF MUSHROOMS AND PÂTÉ, SAUCE MADÈRE

extraordinarily light puff pastry; on Saturdays, the pastry encases a filet of beef cooked with a duxelle of mushrooms and pâté, and served with a sauce Madeira. Jean usually has other specials, too, dictated by availability: fresh trout flown in from Idaho or quail en croûte served with a green peppercorn sauce. There is a good French wine list and an adventurous selection from small California vintners. Reservations are not accepted, but the wait is made painless as possible by an invitation to help yourself from a cask of wine with the compliments of the house.

LE POT AU FEU, 1149 El Camino Real, Menlo Park. Telephone: (415) 322-4343. Hours: 6-10, Tuesday-Saturday. No cards. Reservations not accepted. Wine only. Parking lot in rear.

~~~~~~

Le Menu

Full dinner includes soup, salad, french bread and butter

Les Viandes

* **Le Pot-au-Feu** 7.00
  BOILED BASKET OF BEEF + FRESH VEGETABLES. HOT MUSTARD + GHERKINS

* **La Brochette de Filet aux Champignons** 7.25
  FILET MIGNON & MUSHROOM BROCHETTE

* **Le Tournedos Béarnaise** 8.50
  FILET MIGNON SERVED ON A GOLDEN SLICE OF FRENCH BREAD, TOPPED WITH BEARNAISE SAUCE

* **Le Lapin à la Moutarde** 7.50
  YOUNG BELGIAN RABBIT IN A CREAM + MUSTARD SAUCE

Les Volailles

* **Le Coq au Vin de Napa Valley** 6.75
  CHICKEN IN A RED WINE SAUCE, MUSHROOMS, BACON + CROUTONS

* **Le Canard à l'Orange** 8.00
  CRISP HALF DUCKLING IN AN ORANGE SAUCE 'à ma façon'

La Spécialité de la Maison

* **Le Saumon en Croûte au Beurre Blanc** 7.50
  SALMON IN A PASTRY CRUST, BAKED WITH HERBS AND CREAM. LEMON + BUTTER SAUCE..

San Mateo
LA BONNE AUBERGE
French

$$

One would almost think some capricious power had plucked up this charming inn from the French Alps and plunked it down on bustling El Camino Real. There are high-backed wooden chairs, red and white checkered cloths, candlelight, leaded glass windows, and prints of Paris and the French countryside on the paneled walls. Actually the Alpine overtones come from a previous occupant, The Bavarian Inn. But the kitchen of new owner Philippe del Perugia is decidedly French. He and his wife Huguette, who serves as hostess, came to San Mateo after he had apprenticed in Paris and Montreal. There is a selection of some 15 entrées, plus several daily specials, at truly remarkable prices: $5 for a delightful sauté of chicken livers with a sauce Madeira, to $8.50 for filet mignon with sauce béarnaise. Now, these prices would be modest à la carte, but they include the full dinner—freshly made soup, butter lettuce and mushroom salad, and dessert! And each generous portion is accompanied by a bevy of vegetables—on our last visit, sweet carrots, barely cooked asparagus, al dente beans and thinly sliced potatoes. Among the house specialties are Belgian hare sautéed in white wine, poached salmon with green peppercorn butter, and scallops sautéed with vermouth. If Philippe has baked one of his sensational tarts, splurge and order it à la carte.

LA BONNE AUBERGE, 2075 El Camino Real, San Mateo. Telephone: (415) 341-2525. Hours: 5:30-10, Wednesday-Saturday; 5-9, Sunday. Cards: BA, MC. Reservations advised. Wine only. Street parking.

Palo Alto
LIAISON
Continental

$$

Franco Siccardi and Michael Ghilarducci met while they were waiter and sous-chef (respectively) at Ernie's in San Francisco. In 1976 they opened this modest restaurant in Palo Alto. The interior is dark, a bit stark, with about 50 seats. The menu, however, is quite ambitious, presenting a "liaison" of Italian and French cooking. Appetizers range from escargots to a paper-thin veal tonnato in a creamy mustard sauce. There is pasta aplenty, from a noble fettuccine prepared in a chafing dish at table to gnocchi marinara. Desserts are from both sides of the Alps—mousse to zabaione. Entrées are bi-national, too. The veal here has an Italian accent—piccata, scaloppini, parmigiana. Beef is sauced *à la française*—medallions béarnaise, chateaubriand bordelaise. Lamb might be sauced with mustard in the style of Dijon or roasted in the tradition of Florence. Dinners, with soup or salad, are priced from $6.25 to $10.

LIAISON, 4101 El Camino Real, Palo Alto. Telephone: (415) 494-8848. Lunch: 11:30-2:30, Monday-Friday. Dinner: 5-10:30, Monday-Saturday. Cards: AE, BA, MC. Reservations advised. Full bar service. Parking lot.

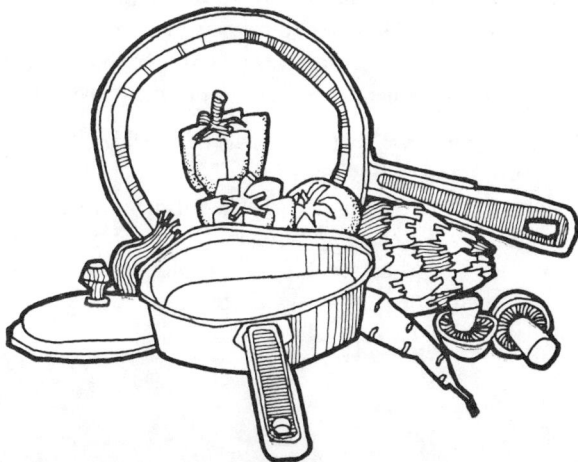

Belmont
PINE BROOK INN
Continental/American

$$

First impressions don't bode well here. If the suburban shopping center locale and the garish neon marquee don't deter you from eating here, the loudspeaker paging dinner guests in the noisy bar probably will. But behind the commercial facade are some pleasant surprises. The dining room, though somewhat crowded and noisy, does have a country feeling—open beams and wood paneling, large windows overlooking garden greenery, picture-pretty tables set with red and white flowered cloths and handsome earthenware pottery. Dinners start with a basketful of freshly baked breads and muffins and a sort of individual salad bar. A chilled bowl of tossed greens and croutons is set on the table with a tray of condiments: marinated beans and beets, slices of German sausage, gefilte fish in sour cream. Mix and enjoy. Then comes a steaming kettleful of fladle soup—julienned strips of beef, German pancakes and vegetables in a rich broth, laced with sherry from a Spanish *bota*. Many of the dinner entrées reflect the German background of owner/chef Klaus Zander (whose international culinary awards are prominently displayed in the restaurant's foyer). We prefer some of the simpler dishes like the shashlik, grilled salmon or salt-coated roast sirloin of beef. Klaus' Austro-Hungarian desserts are a calorie counter's demise. Sunday brunches here offer an exceptionally lavish buffet.

PINE BROOK INN, 1015 Alameda de las Pulgas (Carlmont Shopping Center), Belmont. Telephone: (415) 591-1735. Lunch: 11:30-2:30, Monday-Friday. Dinner: 6-10, Tuesday-Saturday; 5-9, Sunday. Brunch: three seatings at 10:30, 12:15 and 1:45, Sunday. Cards: BA, MC. Reservations are not accepted on Saturday night, but advised at other times. Full bar service. Parking lot.

Influence From The Old Country

Roulades of Beef

THINLY SLICED BEEF STUFFED WITH ONIONS, PICKLES AND
BACON ... BRAISED ... *"IT'S POPULAR AND REAL GERMAN"* . . . 6.75

By Popular Demand "Wiener Schnitzel"

VIENNAS MOST FAMOUS DISH ... PREPARED WITH THE BEST MILK
FED VEAL OBTAINABLE 7.95
A NOT SO LARGE PORTION 6.95

Beef Burgundy In A Pastry Crust

TENDER, JUICY BEEF, ONIONS, MUSHROOMS AND SUCH IN A
BURGUNDY WINE SAUCE 6.25

"Good food is the base for true happiness"

All American Favorite

The finest striploin of beef roasted in a thick coat
of salt and spices to retain it's flavor and juicyness
We revived an *"Old Tradition"* . . . . *Magnificent*
A GENEROUS CUT 8.50
NOT QUITE SO GENEROUS 7.50

The Coachman's Pan

A BONELESS BREAST OF CHICKEN SAUTEED WITH FRESH
MUSHROOMS, GREEN ONIONS ... COMPLETED WITH ARTICHOKE
HEARTS AND BRANDY SAUCE 6.75

A Grilled Salmon Filet   FRESH WHEN IN SEASON

SERVED WITH BEARNAISE SAUCE 7.50
A SMALLER PORTION 6.75

Shashlik on a Spit

MORSELS OF TENDER LAMB, MARINATED WITH FRESH MINT AND
BROILED ON A SKEWER WITH MUSHROOMS 7.95
"It's better to die eating than fighting"   PENNSYLVANIA DUTCH PROVERB

Stuffed Oysters on the Rocks

EASTERN OYSTERS BAKED WITH LAYERS OF FRESH SPINACH,
CRABMEAT, MUSHROOMS AND CHEDDAR CHEESE 8.75
A SMALLER PORTION 7.95

Seafood Harvest

A DELIGHTFUL TRIO OF SALMON FILET, BAKED OYSTER WITH
CRABMEAT AND A BROILED LOBSTERTAIL 9.50
Care for melted butter? Ask us.

Undecided?

We suggest a combination you can't resist. A MEDALLION OF BEEF CUT FROM
BEEF TENDERLOIN with a choice of

FILET OF SALMON 8.25
STUFFED BAKED OYSTER WITH CRABMEAT 8.75
A BROILED LOBSTER TAIL 9.50

Always Available

A GIANT NEW YORK STEAK 8.75
OR NOT SO GIANT 7.50
LITTLE SKEWERED STEAKS CUT FROM BEEF TENDRLOIN 6.75

San Mateo
PIERRE'S WAH YEN
Chinese

$

This used to be a French restaurant. When K.K. Leong and his wife, Eva, started serving Chinese food here, they didn't bother to change the old sign—Pierre's—or the decor. Walls are hung with reproductions of Parisian street scenes, gilded baroque mirrors, crystal sconces. It's a crazy setting for Chinese food, but here the French influence ends. The cooking is decidedly Cantonese, with a few dishes from other provinces such as Szechwan pork, Peking duck and Mongolian lamb. There are old favorites like a superb rendition of gulf prawns in black bean sauce and some unusual concoctions such as chicken with olive seeds and prawns with walnuts. Entrée prices average around $3.50.

PIERRE'S WAH YEN, 211 South San Mateo Drive, San Mateo. Telephone: (415) 343-1144. Hours: 11:30-9, Monday-Saturday. Cards: BA, MC. Wine and beer only. Street parking.

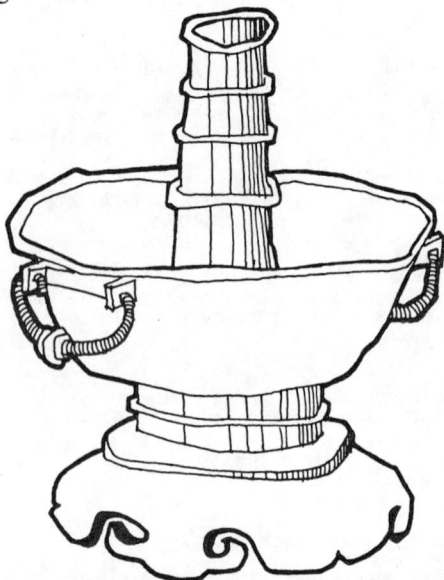

Sunnyvale
TAO TAO CAFE
Chinese (Cantonese)

$$

In the recent fervor over the exotic foods of northern and western China, the cuisine best known to Americans—Cantonese—tends to be overlooked. In fact the Tao Tao Cafe, with its nondescript exterior and commercial-looking interior, could easily be overlooked. But don't. New owner Frank Y. Wong (formerly of Ming's in Palo Alto), runs a first-class Cantonese kitchen with a diversified menu. The shredded chicken salad is a divine way to begin here; spicy poultry is tossed with slivers of scallions, almonds, lettuce and rice vermicelli. The star of the beef dishes here is Tao Tao beef, marinated in a slightly sweet sauce and served over vermicelli. There is a variety of chicken dishes—deep-fried in parchment, stir-fried with fruits or vegetables, or crisply cooked with sesame seeds and a cream sauce. You can order barbecued duck or pressed almond duck off the menu, but we advise ordering the magnificent Peking duck 24 hours in advance; it's served with hearty buns along with scallions, coriander and hoisin sauce for a fantastic "sandwich." The steamed whole cod also must be ordered a day in advance, as must the exotic "dragon and phoenix" chicken, which is spiced chicken layered with Virginia ham. Seek Mr. Wong's advice on ordering here and you probably won't go wrong. Dinners average $5 to $7 per person.

TAO TAO CAFE, 175 South Murphy Avenue, Sunnyvale. Telephone: (415) 736-3731. Lunch: 11 am-2 pm, Monday-Friday. Dinner: 4-10, Monday-Saturday; 4-9:30, Sunday. Cards: AE, BA, MC. Full bar service. Parking lot in rear.

Monterey Area

KILLEEN

Pebble Beach
CLUB XIX
Continental

$$

Located in the exclusive Del Monte Lodge, overlooking the Pebble Beach Golf Course and the rocky Carmel coastline, Club XIX is the watering hole for the famed Crosby tournament. The French dinners here are exceedingly formal and the à la carte prices would put Club XIX in the "$$$" category and then some. We recommend it, however, as one of the most delightful places for lunch or brunch along the entire California coast. The prices are moderate at noontime, the view from the outdoor dining terrace is beautiful and the daily specialties have a Basque touch. We particularly like the creamy, cheesy quiche Lorraine on Wednesdays and the seafood Portofino of wine-sauced scallops and shrimp on Fridays. Lunches are priced around $5 to $6. Lunching at Club XIX also grants you free admission to the 17-Mile Drive; the $4 admission fee is refunded when you pay your meal check!

CLUB XIX, Del Monte Lodge, Pebble Beach. Telephone: (408) 625-1880. Hours: 11-5, 7-10, Tuesday-Sunday. Cards: AE, BA, MC. Reservations advised. Full bar service.

Monterey
CHEZ FELIX
French   **$$**

Dining here is a refreshing change from the typical French restaurant. Chef Felix Roux sparks his menu with imagination. Crab bisque is served with a garlic sauce. Sole is covered with a delicate tomato sauce or poached with other seafood. Fresh Monterey salmon, in season, is wrapped in parchment. Chicken comes sauced with champagne and raisins and cornish hen is roasted with chestnuts. All *très délicieux*. The desserts here are not to be overlooked. A mousse of chestnuts and chocolate is a specialty, as are the fresh fruit tarts. The ambience of a candlelit French country inn, plus a magnificent view of Monterey Bay, makes Chez Felix a most romantic place to dine. À la carte dinners average $10.

CHEZ FELIX, 585 Cannery Row Square, Monterey. Telephone: (408) 373-0556. Hours: 5:30-10; closed Monday. Cards: BA, MC. Reservations advised. Wine only. Street parking.

Merveilles des Mers

FILETS DE SOLE NISSARDE   5.75
covered with a delicate tomato sauce

PAUPIETTES DE SOLE NORMANDE   5.95
poached in seafood sauce

SAUMON DE MONTEREY EN PAPILLOTTE   7.25
(IN SEASON)

SCAMPIS CAMARGUAISE   6.95
for seafood lovers

Volailles et Viandes

POULET SAUTE CYNTHIA   5.80
chicken in champagne & raisin sauce

POUSSIN A LA CEVENOLLE   6.95
cornish hen roasted with chestnuts

GRATIN DE RIS DE VEAU SAUCE DUXELLE   6.50
calf sweetbreads in mushroom sauce

MEDAILLONS DE VEAU BELLE - EPOQUE   7.50
veal in cream & mushrooms

ENTRECOTE MARCHAND DE VIN   8.95
New York cut sirloin, flambe cognac

LA SPECIALITÉE DE FELIX
L'ENTRECOTE DOUBLE AU POIVRE VERT

22 00

Monterey
THE CLOCK
International

$$

If you tire of the quaintness of Carmel or the nostalgia of "old Monterey," a refreshing change is The Clock. Here owners Bob Canon and Jim Stone have created a very personal type of restaurant, an extension of their own artistic and ebullient personalities. You enter through a flower-filled patio and receive a warm greeting at the door from Bob or Jim. Inside, the bar and dining room are colorful, kooky and informal. An incredible number of antique clocks and bright paper collages adorn the resawn redwood walls. The Clock does not aspire to *haute cuisine*, but offers innovative dishes of eclectic national origin. With the dinner, soup and a wedge of lettuce with "precocious" dressing (actually a variation of green goddess) are served. Steaks and lamb chops are also available. The luncheon menu offers homemade soups, sandwiches, crêpes and changing daily specials. Sunday brunch here is a big occasion, with eggs Benedict and Ramos fizzes the specialties. The Clock is one of the peninsula's most reliable restaurants. The Clock is fun. The Clock is also enormously popular, especially with locals. For those who don't want to wait for a seat during peak dining hours, an "early-bird" roast beef dinner is now offered for $6.50 from 5:30 to 7.

THE CLOCK GARDEN RESTAURANT, 565 Abrego, Monterey. Telephone: (408) 375-6100. Lunch: 11:30-2, Monday-Friday. Dinner: from 5:30, nightly. Sunday brunch: 10:30-2. Closed Thanksgiving, Christmas, New Year's. Cards: AE, BA, CB, DC, MC. Reservations advised for dinner. Full bar service. Street parking.

BROILED SALMON STEAK 8.50
THE MONTEREY KING - WINED AND HERBED

BREASTS of CHICKEN DEL SUR 6.75
TOPLESS TEMPTERS STACKED EN CASSEROLE & SOUTHERN SAUCED

VEAL VALLARTA 7.75
SKILLFULLY SEQUESTERED BY SAUCES AND SURPRISES

BROILED FILET TERIYAKI 7.75
BEEF ON A HAWAIIAN HOLIDAY. PERKED IN SOY, GINGERY PINEAPPLE

CREPES de CAMARONES 6.75
SCHOOLS OF TINY CURRIED SHRIMP ENFOLDED LOVINGLY IN
TWO PERFECT CREPES

PORK TENDERLOIN EN BROCHETTE 7.75
LITTLE CUTS ALL IN A ROW - B'BQ THEM AND BROIL-EE-O

CHICKEN LIVER SQUAD 6.50
TRIM YOUNG LIVERS ALL IN A ROW

SCALLOPS del SUIZO 7.50
TENDER SCALLOPS MAKING LOVE WITH LITTLE
SHRIMP IN A LAGOON OF CREAM AND CHEESE.

POULET BICENTENNIAL 6.95
BABY CHICKEN FLAMED IN BRANDY AND SIMMERED
IN MADIERA, MUSHROOMS AND CREAM

FILET of SOLE MEUNIER 7.25
FRESH, SELECT PETRALE SOLE ALL BONED & BUTTERED UP

PECAN PIE, CHEESE CAKE OR MINTED
SHERBERT COINTREAU 1.25

Monterey
ABALONETTI
Italian/Seafood $

If you like squid, ignore the garish tourist restaurants of Fisherman's Wharf and join the line in front of the Liberty Fish Market. Once inside, you'll pass through the market with its counters of fresh squid and other seafood and find yourself in a small, scruffy-looking dining room facing out on the water. If you're tempted to leave at this point, remember the calamari. It's prepared in a number of ways: pounded, breaded and sautéed in butter; stuffed and cooked in tomato sauce; fried Sicilian style with garlic and parsley; or combined with eggplant, tomato sauce and grated cheese. All reasonably priced in the $4 range.

ABALONETTI RESTAURANT, Fisherman's Wharf, Monterey. Telephone: (408) 375-5941. Hours: 11-9; closed Tuesday. No cards. Reservations not accepted. Beer and wine only. Parking in Fisherman's Wharf lot.

Carmel
FLAHERTY'S OYSTER BAR
Seafood $

If you have a hankering for fresh crab, mussels, oysters, you'll find them here. There are only about a dozen stools along a brass-railed, marble-topped counter. The rest of this spic-and-span market with its sparkling blue and white

tiles contains enticing displays of iced fresh seafood. From 11:30 to 2:30 each day, pretty blue napkins dress up the counter and simple luncheon dishes such as cold Maine lobster or snapper Veracruzana are served. Prices are not cheap ($3.50 for six oysters), but the pearls of the sea are as fresh as they can be. Watch for the changing daily seafood specials, too.

FLAHERTY'S OYSTER BAR FISH MARKET, Sixth Street east of Dolores, Carmel. Telephone: (408) 624-0311. Hours: lunch and dinner from 11:30 am, daily. Cards: BA, MC. Beer and wine only.

Carmel
LA BOHÊME
Continental

$$

This small cafe looks like a miniature stage set for a Grimm's fairy tale. A half-timbered cottage in one corner, tables jammed together, hutches filled with blue and white pottery, copper hoods. Inside the cottage, which serves as kitchen, a Belgian chef who has cooked throughout Europe prepares a table d'hôte dinner which is inspired each night by a different country. One night it might be sauerbraten from Munich, the next chicken cooked with truffles and onions from Carcassonne, Sicilian cioppino, or Scotch salmon in a caper sauce. A calendar of menus is printed several months in advance so that you can select your entrée and reserve for that night. The dinners, soup and salad included, are $6.75; a vegetarian dish is also offered along with the evening's entrée. La Bohême is also a sunny, cheerful place for lunch with a hot special each day, as well as open-faced sandwiches, crêpes, omelets, Belgian waffles. The home-made desserts and cheesecake are the pride of the house.

LA BOHÊME, Dolores near Seventh, Carmel. Telephone: (408) 624-7500. Lunch: 11-3, Monday-Saturday; 1-3, Sunday. Dinner: 5-9:30, daily. Sunday brunch: 11-1. Closed Wednesdays in winter. Cards: MC. Wine only. Street parking.

San Juan Bautista
LA CASA ROSA
Early Californian

$

A short detour from Highway 101 will transport you a century back in time to the slow-paced hospitality of Early California. The peaceful mission village of San Juan Bautista looks much like it did 100 years ago, as does the historic Casa Rosa and its antique furniture. Only lunch is served with a choice of two equally delicious entrées: an Early California casserole of corn, cheese and meat, or chicken soufflé (each $3.75). Along with this you will be served a salad with a memorable dressing made from fresh herbs grown in La Casa's garden, and cheesecake or macadamia nut ice cream. For an aperitif, try the ash blonde, a blend of French and Italian vermouths.

LA CASA ROSA, 107 Third Street, San Juan Bautista. Telephone: (408) 623-4563. Hours: 11:30-3:30; closed Tuesday. No cards. Reservations advised on weekends. Beer and wine only. Street parking.

Carmel
LE COQ D'OR
French

$

This tiny, one-room restaurant looks like a European tearoom and is a great favorite of local residents. The cooking of owner-chef Louis Zwahlen is delicious and the prices are most reasonable. Chicken is his specialty and he serves it in

a number of ways: flamed with diced ham and fresh mushrooms, covered with a cream sauce and mushrooms, or served in a simple wine sauce. His chicken livers with mushrooms and sherry is one of the most popular dishes. There are also grilled pork chops or steaks with sherry sauce and fresh salmon in season. Dinner with a soup and a salad mimosa is $4.65 to $7.50 for the steak.

LE COQ D'OR, Mission and Fifth, Carmel. Telephone: (408) 624-4613. Hours: 5:30-9, Wednesday-Monday. No cards. Reservations advised. Wine only.

Carmel
PÂTISSERIE BOISSIÈRE
French $

Eliane and Pierre Boissière earned a formidable reputation for their fine French pastries, but their elegant little salon is much more than a pâtisserie. A nice selection of lunch and dinner specialties, priced from $3.25 to $4, includes coquille St. Jacques, sweetbreads in a pastry shell, curried shrimp and mushrooms, and chicken provençale. This is also a delightful place for an afternoon snack, perhaps quiche, pâté, pork and veal in a pastry roll, or simply camembert, crackers and a glass of wine.

PÂTISSERIE BOISSIÈRE, Mission Street between Ocean and Seventh, Carmel. Telephone: (408) 624-5008. Hours: 10 am-9 pm, Thursday-Tuesday. No cards. Reservations not accepted. Wine and beer only.

Pacific Grove
MAISON BERGERAC
French $$

This turreted gingerbread Victorian is the home of Raymond Bergerac, a very talented and semi-retired French chef. For eight months of the year, Raymond dons his toque three nights a week and prepares the classic country dishes of his native France. Dinners in the beautifully appointed dining room and parlor are served by Madame Bergerac and her children. It is truly like being a guest in a fine French home. Dinners include a freshly made soup, often from home-grown vegetables, and a butter lettuce salad with an outstanding herb dressing. There is also an impressive array of à la carte appetizers: escargots cooked in chablis and herbs, a duck-liver terrine, celeriac with mustard mayonnaise, and fresh Iranian caviar (at $15 per serving!) Desserts include an extraordinarily rich mousse, heavily laced with curaçao. Only French wines are served with a varying house selection at $6 the bottle.

MAISON BERGERAC, 649 Lighthouse Avenue, Pacific Grove. Telephone: (408) 373-6996. Hours: 6-10, Thursday, Friday and Saturday; closed May, June, November and December. No cards. By reservation only. Wine only. Street parking.

Tripe à la Mode Normande 7.00
Honeycomb Tripe Julienne in Calvados

Lapin Rôti au Vin Rouge 9.00
Crock Roasted Carmel Valley Rabbit in Red Wine

Le Bifteck au Poivre Vert de Madagascar 10.00
Medallions of Beef with Green Pepper Corns and Cognac

Cassoulet de Castelnaudary 8.00
Authentic Casserole of White Lingot Beans, Pork, and Sausage

Le Rognon de Veau Dijonnaise 7.00
Kidneys with Shallots and Mushrooms in French Mustard Sauce

Les Escalopes de Ris de Veau Paul Bocuse 8.00
Sweetbreads with Mushrooms in a Light White Wine Sauce

Le Caneton à Ma Façon 10.00
Young Duckling Roasted in the French manner

Carmel
RAFFAELLO
Northern Italian

$$

Tuscany is considered the culinary capital of Italy and the late Raffaello d'Agliano was considered one of the leading Tuscan chefs of his day. For the past decade, Raffaello's wife Amelia and son Remo have been serving exquisite Tuscan food in their tiny, candlelit restaurant in Carmel. Raffaello's is particularly noted for its veal, usually younger and whiter than found in most Northern California restaurants. Pasta dishes are made with homemade egg noodles and the seafood, though limited in selection, is fresh. Dinner prices shown on the facing page include a soup of the day, romaine salad and vegetables. Appetizers and desserts are à la carte. If you plan to dine here on a weekend, reserve several days ahead.

RAFFAELLO, Mission Street between Ocean and Seventh, Carmel. Telephone: (408) 624-1541. Hours: 6-10, Wednesday-Monday. Cards: MC. Reservations required. Wine and beer only. Parking lot.

Pesce *(fish)*

Sogliola Cardinale *(filet of sole poached in Champagne with shrimp)*	7.75
Sogliola Grattnata *(filet of sole with fresh mushroom sauce)*	7.75
Sogliola al Vino Bianco *(filet of sole with white wine sauce)*	7.75
Sogliola di Dover alla Parigina *(filet of sole poached in white wine sauce with herbs rolled & stuffed with prawns)*	7.75
Truites de riviere au bleu *(trout)*	7.75
Aragosta Demidoff *(a delicate flavor of California lobster with the touch of Raffaello)*	9.00

Anatra *(duck)*

Anatra bresata al'arancio - on special order - for 2 *(duck with brandied orange sauce)*	30.00

Pollo *(chicken)*

Petti di Pollo alla Fiorentina *(a superlative dish that will not be forgotten)*	8.00
Petti di Pollo ai Funghi *(tender breast of capon with fresh mushrooms)*	8.00
Pollo alla Cacciatora *(this chicken is prepared from our authentic recipe)*	7.75
Pollo Saltato *(saute with wine & mushrooms)*	7.75
Pollo alla Jerusalem *(with cream sauce & artichoke bottom)*	7.75

Vitello *(Veal)*

Frittura piccata *(with lemon sauce)*	8.25
Vitella alla Pizzaiola *(with a delicate tomato sauce)*	8.25
Scaloppine alla Toscana *(with wine sauce, mushrooms & tomatoes)*	8.25
Vitella alla Milanese *(with fresh mushrooms)*	8.25
Vitella alla Piemontese *(with Fontina cheese & truffles)*	8.75
Vitella alla Romana *(with cheese & prosciutto and mushroom sauce)*	8.75

Sweetbreads

all'Imperatrice *(with cream & wine sauce)*	8.00
Saltato *(sautéed in butter)*	7.75

Alla Griglia *(Beef)*

Tournedos	9.00
Capriccio	9.50

	a la Carte	Dinner *(served with Soup of the day & Romaine salad)*
Pasta *(Homemade Egg Noodles)*		
Cannelloni alla Raffaello	5.00	6.75
Fettuccine alla Romana	5.00	6.75
Tagliatelle alla Bolognese	5.00	6.75
Tagliatelle Pizzaiola	5.00	6.75

153

Carmel
SHABU-SHABU
Japanese

$$

This rustic country inn, located in a shopping plaza, offers one of the state's loveliest experiences in Japanese dining. The two rooms are decorated with rice-paper calendars, hemp rope curtains and peasant-style earthenware. One room offers Western-style seating, while the other contains low tables with cushions on the floor. A large brick fireplace keeps glowing charcoal ready for at-the-table cooking—no electric skillets here! With the dinners come a small plate of tsukemono pickles, a large bowl of dashi broth and a unique salad: icy spinach leaves coated with sesame seeds and a dressing composed of sesame oil, soyu and rice vinegar. The à la carte appetizers are well worth exploring, too—sushi, sashimi, hiya-yakko (cold bean curd covered with bonita flakes and chopped scallions), clams on the half shell and an exquisite tempura. The eleven entrées include a selection of teriyakis, tempura, sashimi and sukiyaki, but one would miss a superb treat by not ordering the specialty from which the restaurant takes its name. Shabu-shabu is traditionally made with beef, but here they also prepare a seafood version, cooked at the table in a charcoal-heated copper pot. Fresh vegetables—spinach, Chinese cabbage, mushrooms—are cooked in the broth along with clams, scallops, shrimps, rock cod and chunks of lobster tail. The cooked morsels are dunked in a creamy mustard sauce or a tangy soy-flavored sauce. At the end of the meal, the cooking broth, now richly seasoned by the seafood, is served in a bowl.

SHABU-SHABU, Mission Street between Ocean and Seventh, Carmel. Telephone: (408) 625-2828. Hours: 6-10, Wednesday-Monday. Cards: AE, BA, MC. Reservations advised. Beer and wine only.

tenpura 7²⁵

Large prawns and vegetables delicately deep-fried in a light and lacy batter.

teriyaki steak 8⁵⁰

10 oz. of rib-eye, char-broiled and glazed with delicious teriyaki sauce.

hibachi steak 8⁵⁰

10 oz. of rib-eye, char-broiled and served with a spicy hot sesame sauce.

teriyaki spareribs 8²⁵

Tender spareribs in teriyaki glaze.

sukiyaki 6⁷⁵

Slices of rib-eye, tofu (soybean cake), shirataki (yam noodle), mushrooms, and fresh vegetables simmered in a seasoned shoyu and sake sauce.

chicken teriyaki 6²⁵

Half tender chicken broiled to perfection and glazed with delicious teriyaki sauce.

sashimi 6⁵⁰

Fresh filet of maguro (tuna) served with wasabi (hot green mustard).

sashimi moriawase 6⁷⁵

A combination of fresh sea delicacies served with wasabi (hot green mustard).

seafood shabu·shabu

A hearty meal of fresh clams, scallops, shrimps, lobster tails, rock cod, and fresh vegetables prepared at your table in the shabu-shabu copper pot. Served with delicious dipping sauces.

22⁰⁰ For two persons

Carmel Valley
THUNDERBIRD
American

$

Dining in a book store is a unique enough experience. But a full buffet dinner of roast beef, curried filet of sole, or chicken supreme—with relishes, blended wild rice, green salad, popovers and desserts for $5.25—is not to be believed in this era. The Thunderbird, one of the state's best-stocked bookstores, encourages browsing and borrowing a book off the shelves to read while you lunch on hearty soup or sandwiches or sip a glass of wine. Recently they moved into a much larger location and added a dramatic new dining room, decorated with natural woods, antique barn lanterns, butcher-block tables and a large stone fireplace.

THUNDERBIRD, Highway One and Rio Road, Carmel. Telephone: (408) 624-1803. Lunch: daily. Dinner: 6-8, Tuesday-Saturday. Cards: BA, MC. Wine and beer only.

Monterey
WHALING STATION INN
Continental

$$

Back in the days when John Steinbeck lived across the street, this was a Chinese grocery store. Several years ago John Pisto spruced it up with dark wood paneling, Tiffany lamps, hanging plants and Early California artifacts and named the restaurant after the old whaling station down the hill. The continental menu features fresh seafood and Pisto is so particular he will only serve crab which he has bought live, to insure its freshness. Portions are enormous and dinners include a fresh artichoke vinaigrette, a soup (the cream of curry is delicious), vegetables and rice with the entrée, bread freshly baked on the premises and salad served after the meal in the European tradition. You won't go away hungry. Seafood aficionados should order the daily special of seasonal fresh fish: perhaps crab cioppino, Monterey salmon, mussels, or sturgeon. Pisto has recently installed an oak-burning barbecue for grilling seafood and has expanded the selection of meats.

WHALING STATION INN, 763 Wave Street, Cannery Row, Monterey. Telephone: (408) 373-3778. Lunch: 11:30-2:30, Monday-Friday. Dinner: 5:30-10, nightly. Closed Christmas, New Year's, Easter. Cards: AE, BA, DC, MC. Reservations advised. Full bar service. Parking lot.

San Simeon Area
GREY FOX INN
Continental

$$

Hungry Hearst Castle visitors take heed: Head south past the touristy highway restaurants to the picturesque village of Cambria. Here in a renovated old house Shirley and Dan Miller serve some of the best food between Carmel and Santa Barbara. The dinner menu varies nightly, but among the four to six entrées there is usually some fresh seafood—salmon from nearby Morro Bay or sole Mornay—and a selection of meat or poultry dishes from Shirley's repertoire of continental recipes. Dinners start with an appetizer (sometimes raw vegetables to be dipped in a honey-curry-sesame sauce), freshly made soup and a salad to which fresh jicama and sprouts are added. The à la carte desserts are well worth the extra investment, especially an incredible peanut cream pie. Lunches are limited to healthful and imaginative sandwiches on homemade bread, and salads. Try the peanut butter/raisin/honey sandwich, surrounded by fresh fruit; or the yogurt salad, another mélange of fresh fruit with almonds, honey and yogurt. Sunday brunches here are also a major event. The menu lists a half dozen omelets (such as the "Oriental" with vegetables and water chestnuts), blintzes, blueberry or potato pancakes, bagels with lox and cream cheese; Parisienne-style French toast and more. Lunches and brunch are under $4; dinners are in the $8 range.

GREY FOX INN, 4095 Burton Drive, Cambria. Telephone: (805) 927-3305. Hours: 11-3, 5:30-9, Tuesday-Saturday; 9 am-2 pm, Sunday. Closed from Monday after Thanksgiving through Christmas Day. Cards: BA, MC. Reservations advised. Wine and beer only. Parking lot.

San Simeon Area
THE HAMLET
Middle Eastern/Continental

$$

A dozen miles south of Cambria (some 20 miles south of Hearst Castle) is a speck on the map called Harmony, population 18. Once a creamery, the small complex of rustic buildings has been spruced up to house craft and antique shops. In a lean-to beside one of the old buildings is an utterly charming restaurant operated by Norm and Maggie Hamlet. It's small and cheerful with a Franklin stove, bright blue tablecloths and jars of fresh flowers on the table. The Hamlets have centered their menu around Armenian family recipes—charcoal-broiled lamb and beef kebabs, spicy soups, pilafs, Middle Eastern breads, lots of fresh fruits. But the cooking roves the continent as well with changing specials such as brisket of beef, moussaka, scampi, stuffed filet of sole. A favorite here, when in season, is fresh king salmon, poached in white wine and served with a butter-cream sauce. Dinners are priced from $4.95 to $7.95 and include soup or salad, breads, cheese and fresh fruit.

THE HAMLET, Harmony. Telephone: (805) 927-3087. Hours: 5-9, Thursday-Sunday; closed during December. No cards. Reservations advised. Wine and beer only.

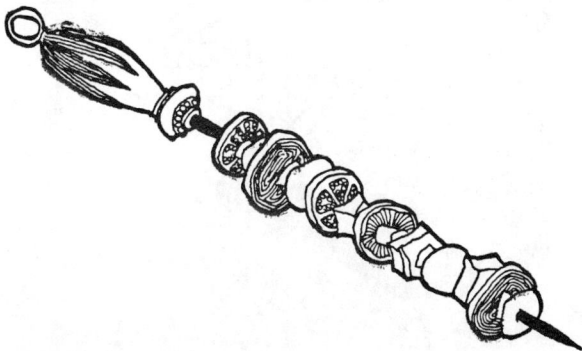

159

Napa/Sonoma Mendocino

Sonoma
DEPOT HOTEL
Continental   **$$**

This century-old hotel and adjoining bar, once owned by General Vallejo, has been smashingly rejuvenated by designer Russell Brown. The gracious bar/living room and dining rooms, refreshingly decorated in white, blue and green, look out onto a flower-filled patio and pool. A few well-chosen antiques and pots of blooming orchids and azaleas are set around the rooms. You feel that you are a guest in an elegant home rather than a patron in a restaurant. Brown, for many years an enthusiastic hobbyist cook, is also the chef at the Depot Hotel. The menu is restricted to a five-course prix fixe dinner for $9.50 with a choice of two to four entrées, appetizer, soup, salad and dessert. The menu consists of whatever Brown feels like creating that day, but often includes chicken, veal or curries. Rabbit makes a regular appearance, as do sweetbreads. Brown takes particular pride in his desserts, which are as delicious as they are unusual: sherry pie, perhaps, a tangy marmalade pie, cheesecake from an old German recipe, or a russe of fresh strawberries.

DEPOT HOTEL, 241 First Street West, Sonoma. Telephone: (707) 938-2980. Dinners: 6-9, Thursday-Sunday. Lunch: Friday, only. Brunch: first Sunday of each month from 10:30-2. Cards: BA, MC. Reservations advised. Wine only. Jackets requested for men. Parking behind restaurant.

Sonoma
AU RELAIS
French $$

Art deco and resawn redwood adorn this refurbished farm-house. Circular windows look out to decks and an outdoor patio with umbrella-covered tables. Over the years we have enjoyed many a leisurely lunch here, although we have had some complaints about dinner service on busy weekends. Owner/chef Harold Marsden is an accomplished cook who brings to Sonoma an expertise gained at some of the fore-most kitchens of Paris and San Francisco. His dinner spe-cialties are shown on the facing page. For luncheon there is a selection of omelets, crêpes and salads, plus an abbrevi-ated choice of the dinner entrées—cassoulet, moussaka, prawns provençale. Both menus offer fresh fish of the day, often poached salmon with a superb Nantua or hollandaise sauce. Soups here are delightful—gazpacho, cold cream of cucumber and spinach, or a lovely shrimp bisque. Luncheon dishes average $3.50 to $5, à la carte.

AU RELAIS, 691 Broadway, Sonoma. Telephone: (707) 996-1031. Hours: 11-9, Monday-Saturday; noon-9 Sunday; closed Tuesday. Cards: BA, MC. Dinner reservations ad-vised. Full bar service. Parking lot.

Appetizers

Coppa	3.00	Oyster Florentine	4.50
*Proscuitto	3.00	Piperade	3.00
*Viande de Grissons	3.00	Escargots Maison	3.50
Paté de Campagne	2.50	Salade Niçoise for Two	6.00
*Lyoner Sausage	3.00	Spinach With Bacon & Croutons for Two	5.00
Tomato Salad	1.75	Tomato Avocado	3.00
	Shrimp Omelette	3.50	

Entrees

Complete Dinners Include: Soup, Salad, Garnish, French Bread, Coffee

Special du Tour Special of The Day.	8.00
Poisson du Tour Fish of The Day.	8.00
Cassoulet Maison Casserole with Pork, Lamb, Beans, Sausage, Duck	8.00
Turkish Mousaka Lamb, Rasions, Nuts, Rice, Barley, Tomato & Zucchini	8.00
Poulet Sauté Gloria Apricots, Walnuts, Cream, Sherry	8.50
Prawns Sauté Provençale Garlic, Tomato, Parsley	9.00
Escalope de Veal Charcutiere Veal Scalops in Cream & Dijon Mustard	10.00
Côtes d'Agneau Marachel Breaded Lamb Chops Saute in Butter	9.50
Canard Normandes or Aux Olives Roast Duckling Cooked in Apples or Olives	9.50
Tournedos Sauté Chasseur Mushrooms, Tomato, Garlic, Sherry	10.50
*Lobster Tail Sauté Nantua 8 oz. Lobster, Saute with Mushrooms Shrimp & Cream	12.00
Carré d'Agneau Aux Poivre Lamb Rack, with Crushed Black Pepper & Cognac (for Two)	24.00

A La Carte Entrees — count One Dollar Less

From The Grill

ALL Served with Sauce Bernaise

Two Cotes d'Agneau	9.50	Prawns Grille	8.50
New York Steak	10.50	Fillet Mignon	10.50

12 Oz. Steak and 8 Oz. Lobster Tail is available if you wish at 15.00

Mendocino Area
LEDFORD HOUSE
Continental

$$

This cozy cottage on the bluffs above the Pacific reeks with charm and atmosphere. And owner Barbara Mastin's cooking is a first-rate rendition of Mediterranean fare—French, Italian, Greek—with her own creative innovations. The cottage is furnished with antiques, mirrors, hanging plants and the tables are set with floral print napkins and fresh flowers. There is a welcoming fire in the dining room, but we prefer to sit on the enclosed veranda and enjoy the spectacular view of the ocean below. The menu changes weekly and offers a choice of six to eight entrées; a typical offering is shown on the opposite page. Fresh vegetables, perfectly cooked, accompany the entrée, as well as freshly baked brioche rolls, a garden salad with a lovely herb dressing, and soup, often a delicious seafood chowder.

LEDFORD HOUSE, Highway One, Little River, 2 miles south of Mendocino. Telephone: (707) 937-0282. Hours: 6-10; days closed vary with season. No cards. Reservations advised. Beer and wine only.

FRESH CAUGHT LOCAL SALMON Today's catch. A large steak served with our own version of béarnaise made with green peppercorns, fresh herbs and crème fraîche $9.50

LOBSTER SOUFFLÉ Layers of baby lobster tails, shallots, mushrooms and herbs with imported Gruyère and Parmesan cheese in an individual soufflé, served with Nantua sauce. $10.50

VEAL CANNELLONI Tender homemade pasta rolled and filled with genuine milk-fed veal, spinach, Ricotta, imported Romano and Parmesan cheeses, and fresh herbs, baked with Allemande or Mornay sauce $9.50

MANICOTTI Homemade spinach pasta rolled and filled with Ricotta, Fontina, imported Romano and Parmesan cheeses and herbs, baked with Mornay sauce and our own meat sauce with imported mushrooms. . $9.50

COSTOLETTINE DI AGNELLO Thick chops from a rack of lamb with a light crust of asiago cheese, served with marsala sauce $9.95

Mendocino Area
LITTLE RIVER CAFE
French

$$

Tucked behind the village market and the post office is a jewel of a little cafe, such as one might find in the country-side of France. There is one small, simply decorated room with only six tables crammed together. Jacques, the owner, prepares exquisite dishes of his native France on a four-burner stove in the postage-stamp kitchen; his American-born wife Debbie does the serving. Throughout the meal both chat with their guests, discussing town news, the weather. The pace is leisurely, civilized. The French touch is pervasive, from the fresh-baked, crusty bread and sweet butter to the brief but carefully chosen all-French wine list. As would be expected, the menu is chalkboard style and ever-changing. A typical dinner starts with a soup, such as potato-based leek, followed by an inspired version of crudités—five or more kinds of julienned fresh vegetables, each marinated in its own tasty dressing. Entrées might be strips of beef in a green peppercorn sauce accompanied with new potatoes; tender fillets of red snapper coated with a delicate mushroom sauce and served with perfectly steamed couscous; chicken glazed with Calvados with white beans alongside; ham in a crusty pastry shell with Madeira sauce; or a spectacular eggplant stuffed with sausage, olives and rice. Desserts are luscious yet simple: perhaps a pot de crème of creamy vanilla ice cream, strawberry preserves and whipped cream. *C'est magnifique.* The prix fixe dinner is $7 to $7.50. A weekend brunch is also served, featuring home-made croissants, omelets, crêpes, etc.

LITTLE RIVER CAFE, Post Office, Highway One, Little River. Telephone: (707) 937-0404. Dinner: seatings at 6:30 and 8:30, Friday-Monday. Brunch: 9-2, Saturday and Sunday. No cards. Reservations advised. Wine only.

Yountville
MAMA NINA'S
Italian

$$

"Do what you do best" is Lee Kline's philosophy of running a restaurant. His place in Cloverdale was noted for homemade pasta and that is what he touts in his new locale in the Napa Valley. In fact you can even look into the glassed-in pasta kitchen and watch the fresh fettuccini, tagliarini, gnocchi and paglia e fieno (a combination of spinach and egg noodles) being made. Mama Nina's also serves tortellini (imported from San Francisco's North Beach), and spaghettini with tomato and basil sauce, plus a changing daily special like cannelloni. There are also some non-pasta entrées—veal piccata, chicken with wine and mushrooms, and scampi sautéed in olive oil and garlic. Kline also prepares unusual Italian desserts like crostata di ricotta, a lemon-flavored torte with a soufflé-like sweet cheese filling. Mama Nina's is housed in a building of contemporary design; you enter through a garden-like bar and luncheon area, with a fireplace set at one end and some tables on an outside terrace. The white walls, hung with a few oil paintings, rise to high wooden ceilings. The wine list contains a good representation of Napa Valley bottlings and a few Italian wines. Entrée prices range from $4 à la carte to $7 for a small dinner (soup or salad), to $10 for a complete dinner which includes an antipasto tray, one of Kline's interesting variations of minestrone, green salad and dessert.

MAMA NINA'S, 6772 Washington Street, Yountville. Telephone: (707) 944-2112. Hours: 11 am-10 pm, daily. Cards: BA, MC. Reservations advised. Wine and beer only at this writing, though application filed for full bar license.

Napa
OLIVER'S
Continental

$$

Oliver's looks and operates like a big-city, downtown restaurant. You won't find quaint wine-country atmosphere here, but you will find some of the finest food in the valley, along with professional yet friendly service. The dining room is very formal—gold banquettes, gold cloths, gleaming crystal and silver, waiters in black tie and a large, dimly lit bar. The kitchen is the domain of co-owner and chef Candido Paz (formerly of Ondine's), who is a master of understatement in the highest classical tradition. Paz' sauces are superb, deceivingly simple in looks but bursting with a subtle symphony of flavors, complementary to but not overpowering the dishes they accompany. Dinner prices include potage du jour and salad; be sure to ask for the house dressing on the latter—one of the most perfectly balanced oil-vinegar-mustard dressings we can remember. Highly recommended here, as appetizer or main course, are the scampi provençale and the sole poached in champagne. Lunches are priced from $2.75 to $5.

OLIVER'S, 1700 Second Street (Robert Louis Stevenson Plaza), Napa. Telephone: (707) 252-4555. Lunch: 11:30-2:30, Monday-Friday. Dinner: 5:30-10, Tuesday-Thursday; 5:30-10:30, Friday and Saturday; 5-9, Sunday. Cards: AE, BA, MC. Reservations advised. Full bar service. Street parking or in adjacent bank parking lot in evening.

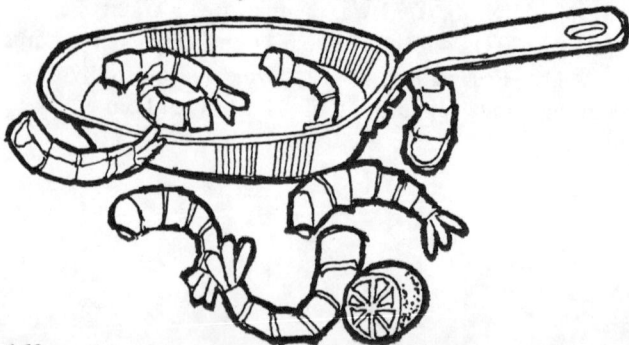

Dinners

FISH IN SEASON **8.50**
The chef will prepare this dish of fish according to his own inspiration.

SCAMPI PROVENÇALE **8.95**
Huge prawns sautéed in butter served with provençale sauce.

FILET OF SOLE OLIVER'S **8.50**
Rolled filet of sole poached in champagne, topped with a light cream sauce.

PAUPIETTES OF SOLE PROVENÇALE **9.50**
Rolled filet of sole with baby shrimp poached in champagne, topped with light cream and tomato provençale sauce.

FILET OF SOLE BRETONNE **8.95**
Sautéed filet of sole with a light butter sauce, shrimp and mushrooms.

CRAB MORNAY **9.75**
Generous portion of Dungeness crab baked in shell with Mornay sauce sprinkled with Romano cheese.

OLIVER'S CREATION **9.75**
This is a combination of scampi provençale and fish in season in light champagne cream sauce.

STEAK AND SCAMPI **11.50**
Petit New York steak presented with scampi provençale.

STEAK AND LOBSTER **11.95**
Petit New York steak presented with fresh lobster.

NEW YORK STEAK **9.50**
A choice cut of sirloin broiled to your taste.

ROAST PRIME RIB — AU JUS **8.50**
A generous cut of carefully aged roast prime rib.

DOUBLE LAMB CHOPS **8.95**
Broiled thick and tender.

SHISH KEBAB ON FLAMING DAGGER AU MADRID **9.50**
Broiled marinated tender cuts of leg of lamb on a spear.

BRAISED SWEETBREADS FINANCIÈRE **8.95**
The classic preparation— imported port wine, fresh mushrooms and black olives.

VEAL SCALLOPINI AU MARSALA **8.95**
The classic preparation — marsala wine and fresh mushrooms.

BREAST OF CAPON SMITANE **8.50**
Breast of capon with a sauce of vodka, fresh mushrooms and sour cream.

Oliver's Gourmet Items

RACK OF LAMB BOUQUETIÈRE (for two) **21.95**
Roast rack of lamb served with vegetables and wilted spinach prepared at your table.

ROAST DUCKLING BIGARADE (for two) **21.95**
A whole duckling basted in the classic fashion with orange sauce.
Served with crisp green salad topped with baby shrimp.

DOUBLE NEW YORK (for two) **21.95**
A specially selected and aged double steak, broiled to luscious perfection and supreme flavor.
Served with a bouquet of vegetables and wilted spinach prepared at your table.

ENTRECÔTE MARCHAND DE VIN **10.50**
New York cut, sautéed, served with a burgundy wine sauce.

STEAK AU POIVRE **10.50**
A choice New York cut with half-cracked pepper, sautéed, flambé en Calvados.

Cheese is, of course, the perfect partner of wine. And now the **Napa Valley Cheese Company** offers a selection of some 175 imported and domestic cheeses to sample along with a selection of Napa Valley wines. A long counter filled with cheeses dominates one wall of the small roadside building; tables set with bright blue cloths and flowers are lined up along the other side. Besides cheese board selections (served with salami, fresh fruit and French bread), there are cheesy sandwiches served with salad, and a selection of entrées like Swiss cheese and onion quiche, teleme cheese omelet or a daily specialty, ranging in ethnic character from quesadillas to fettuccine to cheese blintzes. Lunches here are $3 to $4. (Napa Valley Cheese Company, 7399 St. Helena Highway, between Yountville and Oakville. Telephone: (707) 944-8333. Lunch: 11-5, daily. Cards: BA, MC. Wine and beer only. No smoking allowed.)

Another good selection of cheese, though not so diverse, is to be found at **Bon Appétit**, a country cafe as French as Burgundy's Côte d'Or. Tables are covered with red-checkered oilcloth, French wine-country posters line the walls and a long deli counter contains not only cheese but a selection of owner Richard Delisle's homemade pâtés, quiches, chocolate mousse and feather-light cheesecake. Delisle also offers sandwiches and superb soups from a repertoire of French recipes. Bon Appétit's "francophilia" stops with the wines. There is a fine selection of Napa and Sonoma bottlings and a daily wine tasting session from 3 to 5 pm. You can lunch here for $2 to $3 or take the food out for a wine country picnic. (Bon Appétit, 4120 St. Helena Highway, between Napa and Yountville. Telephone: (707) 252-7311. Hours: 11:30-4, Monday-Saturday. Cards: BA, MC. Wine only.)

Yountville's Vintage 1870, a complex of shops housed in an old winery, offers two charming and informal spots for lunching indoors or outside. **The Chutney Kitchen** fea-

tures sandwiches the likes of smoked salmon with cream cheese or smoked tongue, salads, and a lovely fresh soup, which is very often a delicious cream of zucchini. They also serve a Sunday brunch with a choice of omelets accompanied with fresh fruit and cheese biscuits. One of the best charcoal-broiled hamburgers in the valley is to be found at **Vintage Cafe**, also in Vintage 1870. Sandwiches, grilled frankfurters and an interesting selection of blended coffees are available as well. Menu items at both places are in the $2 to $3 range. (Chutney Kitchen, Vintage 1870, Yountville. Telephone: (707) 944-2788. Lunch: noon-5; closed Monday. Sunday brunch: 10:30-12:30. Vintage Cafe, Vintage 1870, Yountville. Telephone: (707) 944-2614. Lunch: 10:30-4; closed Monday. Dinner: 5-9, weekends. No cards. Wine and beer only: Vintage Cafe has full bar service 5-9, weekends.)

Central Valley

Sacramento
CHINA CAMP
Chinese/Californian

$$

California's gold rush era has been recreated in Sacramento's Old Town, a restoration of river-front buildings that once housed D. O. Mills' bank, Leland Stanford's dry goods store and other pioneer businesses. Most intriguing of the new restaurants is China Camp, built by Chinese restaurateur Frank Fat in tribute to his countrymen's contributions to California history—and California cuisine. Rough timber interiors, bits of old railroad and mining equipment, and photographs recall the past. As Chinese cooks did in the mining camps of yore, China Camp adapts Oriental cooking methods to foods available in the West, often by marinating meats, seafood and fowl with Chinese herbs and sauces. From Chinese smoke ovens come marinated rack of lamb and Western spareribs. From the wok come stir-frys of lobster or pepper steak with black bean sauce, or chicken with black mushrooms. Then there is a host of unique China Camp specialties: poached butterfly shrimp, brandy chicken, petrale sole served with sweet-sour sauce and almonds and the "camp house special," a Cornish game hen simmered in a blend of 12 herbs and spices, then fried to a crackling gold and served with orange sauce. Dinners ($4.95 to $9.95) include soup or green salad with hot sourdough bread from San Francisco. Lunches (under $4) include some of the Chinese-Western specialties, as well as more traditional salads and sandwiches, garnished with fresh fruits.

CHINA CAMP, 1015 Embarcadero, Sacramento. Telephone: (916) 441-7966. Lunch: 11:30-2, Monday-Friday. Dinner: 5:30-10:30, Monday-Thursday; 5:30-11, Friday and Saturday; 4-9:30, Sunday. Cards: AE, BA, MC. Reservations advised. Full bar service. Parking lot.

Sacramento
FIREHOUSE COURTYARD
Californian

$

On a simmering hot Sacramento day, the Courtyard is like an oasis. Large shade trees form an umbrella over the brick courtyard, where a splashing fountain creates an aura of coolness. Legislators and localites crowd the outdoor area, a part of the Firehouse Restaurant in Sacramento's historic Old Town. You'll find salads such as "avocado undecided" (with crab, tuna or shrimp) or fresh spinach, plus omelets, sandwiches and entrées with an Early California accent. There is San Francisco Joe's special, Hangtown fry and Captain John Sutter's devil bones (meaty beef bones with sauce). On cooler days, dine inside under a massive stained glass dome, originally from the old courthouse in Stockton. Luncheon dishes are priced at $2.50 to $4.50.

FIREHOUSE COURTYARD, 1112 2nd Street, Sacramento. Telephone: (916) 442-4773. Hours: 11:30-2, Monday-Saturday. Cards: AE, BA, MC. Reservations advised. Full bar service. Parking lot.

Sacramento
FUJI SUKIYAKI
Japanese

$

In this tranquil little restaurant, the Fujita family serves a large and interesting array of Japanese foods at amazingly low prices. For $2 to $4 you may choose from 18 dishes which range from teriyakis, sukiyaki and tempura to chicken mizutaki, oysters cooked with vegetables and soybean paste, or beef broiled with a hot chili sauce. Included in the price are rice, a bowl of clear broth, pickled vegetables and green tea. For under $2, there is a selection of hearty donburi dishes (meats and vegetables served over rice) and udon (Japanese noodle dishes), also served with pickled vegetables and tea. Fuji is one of the few restaurants we know of to serve fresh eel.

FUJI SUKIYAKI, 2422 13th Street, Sacramento. Telephone: (916) 446-4135. Cards: AE, BA, MC. Reservations advised. Beer and sake only. Street parking.

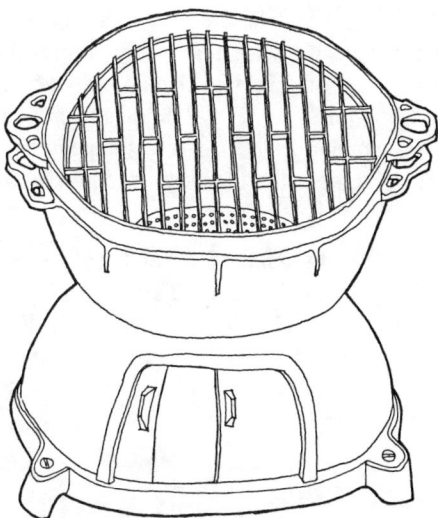

Vacaville
THE NUT TREE
Californian

$$

Originally a roadside fruit stand, later a rustic cafe, The Nut Tree is now a sort of mini-Disneyland with its own airport, miniature railroad and complex of shops. Despite the commercialism and relatively high prices, The Nut Tree serves food of top quality representative of California's multi-ethnic history. The dining room looks like a dramatic greenhouse with a ceiling about three stories high, the interior space broken up by bright-colored canopies and gigantic tree-plants. Among the entrées is one of the finest cornhusk tamales in the state, Chinese stir-fry dishes, barbecued spareribs and a selection of shrimp, fruit or vegetable salad platters. Small loaves of delicious freshly baked bread accompany each entrée along with an abundance of fruits or vegetables; portions are generous. With the complete dinners, a pineapple appetizer, hot or cold soup and dessert are included. The latter are sensational: pumpkin pie with whipped cream, plum pudding, chess pie with walnuts, homemade cakes, etc. The Nut Tree also has an excellent all-California wine list with reasonably priced vintage varietals from many of the state's small wineries. Luncheon entrées range from $5 to $8, full dinners from $8 to $10. If you'd like a simpler, quicker and less expensive meal, The Coffee Tree, across the highway, offers the same high quality.

THE NUT TREE, Interstate 80, Nut Tree (Vacaville). Telephone: (707) 448-6411. Hours: 7 am-9 pm, Sunday-Thursday; until 10 pm, Friday and Saturday. Cards: BA, MC. Reservations advised Monday through Saturday; not accepted on Sundays and holidays. Wine and beer only. Parking lot.

Sacramento
THE RAM
Continental

$$

This is one of Sacramento's most popular restaurants, night and day, for a number of reasons. The food is good, the helpings hearty and the prices reasonable; and locals usually are assured of running into someone they know, for all Sacramento seems to turn up here sooner or later. But the prime factor of the Ram's success is the diligence and watchfulness of owner Richard Hart, who greets you at the door and is never far away if you need him. The menu includes both Basque and Italian fare with a smattering of entrées from other parts of the world—even prime rib with Yorkshire pudding. Lamb and beef dishes are excellent here and the changing daily special should not be overlooked. Dinner prices include a tureen of homemade soup, green salad, French "herder" bread, country-style potatoes and vegetables. Lunch at the Ram features sandwiches, salads and a few hot dishes, priced under $4. Even the Parisian steak sandwich, a New York cut broiled with sautéed onions and peanut butter (!) is only $3.50. For the night owl a "mini-menu" is served from 10:30 until 1 am: omelets, sandwiches, cannelloni and eggs Benedict are but a few of the late-night choices.

THE RAM, 630 Watt Avenue, Sacramento. Telephone: (916) 481-4910. Hours: 11 am-1 am; closed Sunday and major holidays. Cards: AE, BA, MC. Reservations required. Full bar service. Parking lot.

Sacramento
RESTAURANT LA SALLE
French

$$

While stationed in France with the army, Dick Vickers became so enamored of French cooking that he stayed on to study *la haute cuisine.* Eventually he started cooking epicurean dinners at the historic Sutter Club in Folsom, attracting a clientele from Sacramento and even San Francisco who were seriously interested in food. Finally Vickers realized a long ambition and, with his wife Annik as hostess, opened a first-class restaurant in Sacramento. Now several years old, La Salle mellows and improves with age as Vickers carefully enlarges his menu and builds his extensive list of French wines. In addition to the printed menu items, Vickers prepares each evening a traditional specialty from one of various regions of France: perhaps bouillabaisse, couscous or tripe. Among the dessert selections are crêpes suzettes and a wicked concoction called chantilly cordial, a velvety ice cream so generously laced with liqueurs that he refuses to sell it to persons under 21.

RESTAURANT LA SALLE, 943 Howe Avenue, Sacramento. Telephone: (916) 483-7977. Hours: from 6 pm, Tuesday-Saturday. Cards: BA, MC. Reservations advised. Full bar service. Parking lot.

Escargots de Bourgogne
OR
Appetizer La Salle
please ask your waiter for today's specialty
$3.75

Dinners

All dinners include:
Potage du Jour, Salad Maison, Potato, Fresh Vegetables,
Bread and Sweet Butter

Onion Soup Gratinée (10-20 minutes) with dinner order $1.25

Special Fish of the Day................... $7.75

Coquilles Saint·Jacques................ $8.00
scallops with tiny shrimps in a light cream sauce

Cherry Stone Clams à la Charentaise........ $8.00
steamed and bathed in a white wine, shallot and cream sauce

Sea Bass en croûte...................... $8.00
with a spinach and mushroom stuffing

Frog Legs Marennes..................... $8.75
lightly sautéed in butter with pine nuts, herbs and garlic

> Special Regional Dish............... $8.50
> Please ask your waiter for today's selection

Sweetbreads Emmanuelle............... $8.75
lightly sautéed with fresh mushrooms in special sauce

Roast Duckling Quatre·Saisons.......... $9.25

Rack of Lamb Rochelle (for 2) price per person.... $10.50

Tournedos Gourmandise................. $9.75
medallion of filet mignon with fresh crushed pepper,
shallots and meat glaze sauce

Chateaubriand Maître d'Hotel (for 2) price per person. $10.50

Fillet of Beef Wellington (for 2) price per person.. $10.75

179

Sacramento
WULFF'S
French $$

One would never believe that behind this nondescript facade in a shopping center is a charming replica of a French countryside inn with antique sideboards, beamed ceilings, tiled floors and pewter accents. Former engineer Horace Wulff and his wife Helen opened Wulff's in the early 1970s so that he could devote full time to his hobby of cooking. A loyal clientele developed and this restaurant is now regarded by many as Sacramento's most outstanding dining experience. Yet Horace keeps in practice with his slide rule by keeping the prices down. In addition to the regular menu items, there is always a special or two. The Wulffs are particularly proud of their quail; other specials include choucroute garni, veal sweetbreads, oysters Mornay, couscous and tripe à la mode de Caen. At lunchtime simple French fare, such as crêpes and omelets, is served.

WULFF'S, 2333 Fair Oaks Boulevard, Sacramento. Telephone: (916) 922-8575. Lunch: 11:30-2, Tuesday-Friday. Dinner: 6-9:30, Tuesday-Thursday; 6-10:30, Friday and Saturday; closed last two weeks in July. Cards: AE, BA, MC. Reservations advised. Full bar service. Parking lot.

Wulff's Restaurant

Soupe du Jour
Salade

Suprême de Volaille en Croûte Breast of chicken in crust	6.50
Ris de Veau à la Crème Sweetbreads	7.10
Paupiettes de Veau Stuffed veal slices on rice	6.85
Crêpes à l'Indienne Curried lamb in crepes	6.15
Filet de Sole Amandine Petrale sole with almonds	6.85
Coquilles St. Jacques à la Parisienne Scollops with mushroom in wine sauce	7.10
Lapin Sauté au Vin Blanc Rabbit in white wine sauce	7.75
Canard à la Crème Duck in a sauce of natural juices and cream	7.95
Rôti de Porc à la Robert Roast Pork in sauce Robert	6.65
Tournedos with mushrooms in Madeira Sauce	8.35
Top Sirloin Steak	7.95

Coffee, tea or Sanka   40
Tea imported from Fortnum & Mason, Ltd.
The price of alcoholic beverages includes sales tax.

181

Hanford
IMPERIAL DYNASTY
French/"Chinoise"

$$$

Hanford is a small agricultural community of 15,000 in the heartland of the San Joaquin Valley, some 40 miles off the route from San Francisco to Los Angeles. Yet this sleepy town has become a Shangri-la for a pilgrimage of epicures from all over the country. Their temple is the Imperial Dynasty, their high priest is chef Richard Wing and they pay homage to a unique cuisine that blends French cooking with Chinese. Wing was born in Hanford, where his family has operated a Chinese restaurant for three generations. After studying international relations, he joined the foreign office of the U.S. Department of State as aide to General George Marshall. Wing traveled widely, discovering the foods of the world and acquiring an expertise in preparing them, especially Chinese and French cuisines. Returning to Hanford, he opened the Imperial Dynasty where he has combined the basic concepts of the world's two greatest cooking traditions into a high form of culinary art which he calls "continental Chinoise." A casual visitor to the Imperial Dynasty, ordering a complete dinner from the printed menu ($8 to $15), would probably be pleased but might wonder what all the hoopla is about. To experience fully Richard Wing's culinary genius, one must organize a party of at least six persons and order days or weeks in advance the "Imperial Dynasty Gourmet Dinner." For $30 per person you will experience an eight- or nine-course banquet unlike any other gastronomic adventure. The menu is rarely the same, but a typical menu is reproduced on the following page. The wine cellar of the Imperial Dynasty is on a par with its food. It abounds with great bottles like Romanée Conti, Bernkastler Doctor, Montrachet, great clarets and California cabernets dating back to the fifties.

IMPERIAL DYNASTY, China Alley, Hanford. Telephone: (209) 582-0087. Hours: 4:30-10:30; closed Monday. Cards: AE. Reservations advised. Full bar service. Parking lot.

IMPERIAL DYNASTY

Typical Gourmet Dinner: $30

SAUMON ET FILET MIGNON STEAK TARTARE
Honeydew melon topped with ribbons of fresh raw salmon and
filet mignon, laced with sweet onion rings, garnished with grated
egg whites, Chinese snow moss and flakes of cilantro.

ESCARGOTS À LA IMPERIAL DYNASTY
Snails cooked with butter and garlic, cashew purée, shallots,
herbs and chablis, garnished with thinly sliced onions.

CONSOMMÉ RICHE DE CHUKKAR AUX HASMA
A clear chukkar broth enriched with hasma (thymus glands of frogs),
Chinese mushrooms and lobster quenelles flavored with cilantro.

PETITS HOMARDS AU ABALONE À LA DIABLE
Poached trout fillets, blanketed by sautéed abalone,
covered with butterflied prawns and topped with a
spinach leaf, quickly fried in peanut oil.

SUPRÈMES DE PIGEONNEAUX À LA CHINOISE
Fresh roasted squab served on a bed of wild rice, pine nuts,
almonds, mushrooms, water chestnuts, garnished with mandarin orange.

ESCALOPES DE VEAU PÉRIGOURDINE
White veal in a sauce of truffles and almonds, accompanied by
eggplant fried golden in sesame oil.

SALADE DE ROMAINE-KIWI
Crisp romaine lettuce and slices of kiwi fruit
with a light French dressing

POMMES AU FOUR
À LA CRÈME DE FROMAGE GRAND MARNIER
A large apple, baked with spices, and stuffed with cream cheese,
topped with whipped cream laced with Grand Marnier

FROMAGE DE MUNSTER
DEMITASSE

Mother Lode

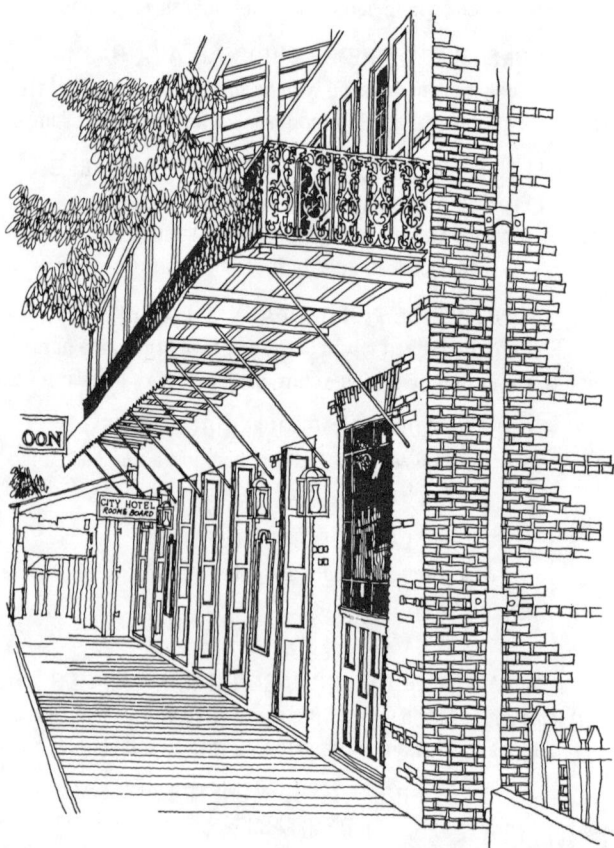

Jackson
ARGONAUT INN
Continental

$$

Assisted by a group of young artists, Katharine Sinclair has transformed the old headquarters of the Argonaut Mine into a homey, antique-filled inn and art center. Mrs. Sinclair, a creative and versatile cook, prepares several entrées each night from her large repertoire of original variations on classic themes. There is usually an imaginative version of chicken (her favorite meat), a simple selection like pork grandmère or leg of lamb, and something for vegetarians—either fish, a quiche, or mushrooms en cocotte. Curries make a frequent appearance, too. Dinners, priced in the $6 range, include a homemade soup and a green salad served after the entrée. Mrs. Sinclair's rich desserts are $1 extra. Before dinner, aperitifs are served in front of the big stone fireplace or on the deck overlooking the wooded hills. The dining room looks like a private home, with tables set with family china, silver and linen. Service is by the young artists-in-residence.

THE ARGONAUT INN & ART CENTER, Vogan Toll Road, Jackson. Telephone: (916) 223-1475. Hours: 6:30-9, Tuesday, Wednesday, Friday and Saturday; 4-7, Sunday. No cards. Reservations advised. Wine only. Easy parking.

Sutter Creek
THE BRINN HOUSE
Sandwiches and Soup

$

Built in 1857 by gold rush merchant Morris Brinn, this old house was charmingly restored in 1974 by Salvatore and Earlene Evola. Only lunch is served here—simple fare of sandwiches, salads and a delicious minestrone. And what they do, they do exceptionally well. Thin slices of ham, turkey, pastrami or roast beef are piled about an inch thick on dark bread or French rolls. Bowls of homemade mustard sauce and creamy horseradish accompany them. Sand-wiches are fairly priced around $2.25. The pies and cheese-cake are delicious, too.

THE BRINN HOUSE, 77 Main Street, Sutter Creek. Tele-phone: (916) 267-5312. Hours: 11:30-3:30, daily. No cards. Reservations not accepted. Wine only.

Auburn
BUTTERWORTH'S
English/Continental $$

In a restored Victorian home perched on a hillside above Auburn, an English couple are doing their best to disprove the myth that the English are notoriously poor cooks. Though prime rib with Yorkshire pudding is the specialty of the house, the menu spans the continent to include abalone almadine, Bordeaux beef, shrimp Coronado, mari-nated lamb chops and quail in season. Dinners include a freshly made soup (perhaps borscht, minestrone, cheddar cheese or split pea), salad with their own "Savonna goddess" dressing, and superb homemade bread. Mrs. Butterworth also makes her own pastries. Luncheons offer a choice of 10 entrées—Welsh rarebit, steak and kidney pie, avocado stuffed with crab salad—plus a wide assortment of unusual sandwiches. For Sunday brunch there is a choice of five or six dishes ranging from Szechwan duck and shrimp/ham jambalaya to crêpes and quiche, all served with home-baked sweet rolls and a champagne fruit cup. In short, Butter-worth's offers some of the finest food between Sacramento and Lake Tahoe. Dinners are priced from $6.50 to $12.95, lunches from $2.25 to $4.50, and brunch from $3 to $4.75.

BUTTERWORTH'S, 1522 Lincoln Way, Auburn. Tele-phone: (916) 885-0249. Lunch: 11-2, Tuesday-Saturday. Dinner: 5-9, Monday-Thursday; 5-10, Friday and Saturday; 3-8, Sunday. Brunch: 11:30-2:30, Sunday. Cards: AE, BA, MC. Dinner reservations advised. Wine and beer only.

Columbia
CITY HOTEL
French

$$$

This elegantly restored, 120-year-old hotel is truly a journey into yesteryear. The gracious high-ceilinged dining room is a study in classic understatement, a serene setting for the magnificently appointed tables set with cut-glass goblets, graceful wine glasses of varying sizes, flowered service plates, small brass hurricane lamps and even silver napkin rings on the sparkling white napery. And for this historic gold town, the menu is a bonanza, more like that of a first-rate French restaurant in a metropolitan city. So it should be: The chef was formerly at Ernie's in San Francisco. Among our favorite dishes here are limestone lettuce salad with mushrooms, French onion soup, poached chicken Cynthia in a superb sauterne sauce laced with orange segments and mushrooms, sweetbreads in a tantalizing champagne sauce and a first-rate chateaubriand with béarnaise. The City Hotel (which also has bedrooms upstairs for overnight guests) is a unique operation. The young waitresses in their long, last-century dresses and the waiters and busboys in the black-tied formal garb are not the inexperienced college students usually found at resort hotels. They are all serious students of the Hospitality Management program at Columbia Junior College, which operates the hotel as an on-the-job training facility. A complete dinner from the à la carte menu will add up to $12 or $15, but is well worth it.

CITY HOTEL, Main Street, Columbia. Telephone: (916) 532-1479. Hours: 5:30-9:30, Tuesday-Saturday. Cards: BA, MC. Reservations advised. Full bar service. Parking lot.

Coloma
VINEYARD HOUSE
Country Style/American

$

Built in 1878, the Vineyard House was once a lavish, 19-room residence surrounded by 500 acres of vineyards. Don't be deterred by the rumor that the house is haunted by the ghost of the original owner, who reportedly starved himself to death in the basement. There is nothing ghostlike about the cheerful, homey dining room, which was lovingly restored by new owners in 1975. A fire burns in the Franklin stove. Genuine kerosene-burning lamps flicker on tables topped with brown and white checkered cloths. Dishes and flatware are a mishmash of patterns from a myriad of periods, but this only adds to the charm. Actually, dining here is like a visit to grandma's country home in some bygone era. And you certainly will not starve. The food is old-fashioned, country-style, not always perfect, but always hearty and homemade. Large pots of fresh soup and big bowls of salad are set on the table and you serve yourself. The bread is freshly baked. Among the entrées is chicken with dumplings like grandma used to make—an enameled saucepan of fowl simmering in gravy and topped with a two-inch layer of biscuit dumpling. Other entrées include German sausage simmered in beer and served with a bowl of buttered noodles, shrimp Newburg and beef stroganoff. And the prices are also more like yesteryear with complete dinners ranging from $4.25 for a vegetarian plate to $8.25 for a 14-ounce New York steak. À la carte desserts are old-fashioned, too: bread pudding, deep-dish apple pie and pecan pie—made with walnuts.

VINEYARD HOUSE, Coloma. Telephone: (916) 622-2217. Hours: 6-9, Wednesday and Thursday; 6-10, Friday and Saturday; 3-9, Sunday; open daily for lunch and dinner during the summer. Cards: AE, BA, MC. Wine only.

Lake Tahoe Area

North Lake Tahoe
CANTINA LOS TRES HOMBRES
Mexican

$

Locals unanimously agree that Tahoe's best Mexican food is to be found in this bustling cantina. The setting is hip, with interior shingles, driftwood assemblage, hanging ferns, booths covered with bright awning stripes, stained glass windows. Complete dinners, under $5, include soup or salad, rice and beans, and a choice of entrées ranging from chile verde (pork in green chili sauce) to steak picado (pieces of beef sautéed with onions, peppers and tomatoes). The most popular—and most economical—dishes here, however, are the burritos, especially the hearty "hombre," stuffed with rice, beans and beef colorado, topped with red chili sauce and melted cheese. A meal in itself for only $3.

CANTINA LOS TRES HOMBRES, 8751 North Lake Boulevard, Kings Beach. Telephone: (916) 546-4052. Hours: 5-10:30, daily. Cards: BA, MC. Wine and beer only in winter; full bar service, March-November.

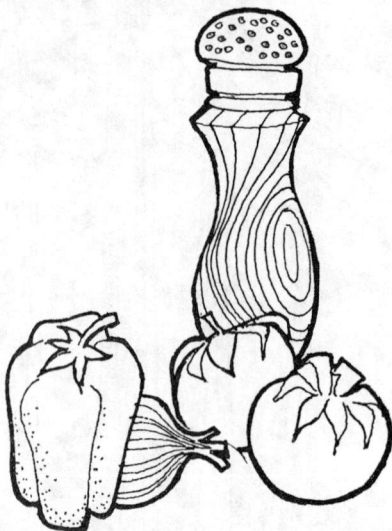

South Lake Tahoe
CHEZ VILLARET
French

$$

From the outside, this little house on the highway, in a strip of nondescript motels, would never cause you to stop. Once inside, *voilà*–you think you have been transported to a French country inn. The small dining room is charmingly decorated with provincial flowered wallpaper and formally set tables. The menu is à la carte here, but the appetizers are reasonable considering what you get. The chef's liver pâté, enhanced by a Cumberland sauce, is delicious, as is the rich lobster bisque. The salade maison is an extravagant concoction of butter lettuce, bay shrimp and tomatoes with a lovely light dressing. The veal here is white and served as a chop, bathed in a creamy sauce with minced wild mushrooms. We also like the scampi; the shrimp are of good size and expertly prepared with lots of garlic. Chef Ray Villaret and his partner, Belgian-born Eddie Pevenage, carry on the tradition of fine French cooking. À la carte entrées range in price from $5.50 for lasagne verde to $19.95 for rack of lamb for two.

CHEZ VILLARET, Highway 89 and 15th Street, South Lake Tahoe (north of the Y). Telephone: (916) 541-7868. Hours: 6-11, Tuesday-Sunday. Cards: AE, BA, MC. Reservations advised. Beer and wine only.

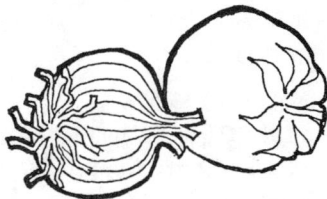

South Lake Tahoe
CHRISTIANIA INN
Continental/American

$$

Nestled in the pines, high above Lake Tahoe, the Christiania Inn provides a comfortable respite of leisurely dining, seemingly worlds away from the neon jungle of the South Shore casino complex. In recent years the inn had become slightly scruffy, but a major face lifting in the winter of 1977 transformed it into a little jewel of a European inn such as one might find in the Alps of Switzerland or Austria. Both the comfortable bar/lounge and dining room have stone fireplaces and a view of the lower slopes of the Heavenly Valley ski area, at the base of which Christiania is located. The menu is basically continental with a few Western touches like country-style ribs. Dinners start with a bowl of soup and freshly baked bread. In the European tradition a salad is served after the entrée, followed by a selection of fruit and cheeses. There are à la carte pastries as well made by the Christiania's own pastry chef. Manager Patrick Robinson has assembled one of the finest wine cellars at Lake Tahoe. There are some 2,000 bottles, which include most of the notable offerings of California's small vintners, as well as imports from Europe. A unique feature is the service of California premium varietals by the glass, a different selection every evening, to give guests an opportunity for some vinous exploration without investing in a full bottle. The Christiania's new wine cellar may be reserved for private parties of 24 persons.

CHRISTIANIA INN, 3918 Saddle Road (top of Ski Run Boulevard), South Lake Tahoe. Telephone: (916) 544-7337. Hours: 6:30-10:30, daily. Cards: AE, BA, DC, MC. Reservations advised. Full bar service. Parking lot.

The First Course

Coquille St. Jacques $ 3.75
Large, firm scallops in a white wine cream sauce, bordered by a piping of whipped potatoes, then baked in a cockle shell.

Scampi Parisienne $ 3.75
A trio of large prawns, sauteed, then drawn in a butter sauce with a mild touch of garlic, selected herbs and savory spices.

Stuffed Mushrooms $ 2.50
Giant mushroom caps filled with a flavorful mixture of tangy cheese, squawbread crumbs and a delicate seasoning of garlic and herbs.

Oysters Rockefeller $ 3.75
Eastern oysters in the shell, cloaked with pureed spinach, dusted with Parmesan cheese, basted with butter and baked until plump.

French Fried Zucchini $ 2.50
Garden fresh Zucchini, quartered and bathed in a buttermilk batter and deep fried until deliciously crunchy.

Imperial Beluga Caviar $12.50
For that very special occasion! The finest of imported Russian caviar, served iced, and accompanied by rye toast points, hard boiled eggs, chopped onions and sour cream.

The Main Course

Veal Oscar *(this should have a fine Riesling wine)*   **$10.00**
Medallions of tender milk-fed veal, sauteed in creamery butter, dressed with King Crab meat and asparagus spears, then covered with a velvety Sauce Bernaise. Served with fresh vegetable.

Roasted Country Duckling *(Petite Sirah, Chateauneuf du Pape wines)*   **$ 8.50**
One half North Country Duckling roasted to a honey-glazed golden brown while simmering in our orange sauce. Served with a mixture of organic grains and fresh vegetable. Sauce a L'Orange.

Lamb Chops *(Zinfandel, Beaujolais wines are suggested here)*   **$ 9.50**
Tender French-cut double rib lamb chops broiled to pink tenderness. Served with petite parslied potatoes and garden vegetable. Mint garnish.

Boeuf Bourguignon *(Cabernet Sauvignon, Bordeaux wines)*   **$ 7.75**
A perfect example of hearty French country cooking. Tender chunks of top sirloin of beef simmering in a Burgundy wine sauce, accompanied by mushrooms, pearl onions, carrots, celery and potatoes. Served with our mixed grains.

Mountain Trout "Jeremiah" *(Chardonnay, Puilly Fuisse, Riesling wines)*   **$ 6.75**
Boned Rainbow trout, stuffed with a cornbread dressing, shrimp, crabmeat and selected herbs, then sauteed in a butter sauce and served with fresh seasonal vegetable and our organic grains.

Scampi *(Chardonnay, Pouilly Fuisse, Bordeaux Blanc wines)*   **$ 8.00**
Tender large prawns, butterflied, then delicately sauteed in a mild garlic-butter sauce. Served with fresh vegetable and mixed grains.

English Country-Style Beef Ribs *(Cabernet Sauvignon, Bordeaux, Burgundy wines)*   **$ 7.50**
Thick, meaty beef ribs, barbecued slowly over charcoal while being basted with our own specially blended sauce. Served with our mixed grains and fresh seasonal vegetable.

Beef Wellington *(Cabernet, Bordeaux wines for this)*   **$10.75**
A filet cut from the heart of the tenderloin, brushed with a delicate mushroom paté, wrapped in a flaky pastry crust, and baked until golden brown. Served with a rich Sauce Bordelaise and accompanied by organic mixed grains and fresh vegetable.

Aged Top Sirloin Steak *(Late Harvest Zinfandel, Chateauneuf du Pape wines)*   **$ 9.50**
A 3/4 pound center cut of our choicest top sirloin dry aged to give it flavor. Charcoal broiled to your taste. Served with garden fresh vegetable and mixed grains.

Peppercorn Steak *(Cabernet Sauvignon, Pinot Noir, Bordeaux)*   **$10.50**
Center cut dry aged top sirloin steak pressed with coursely ground black peppercorns and pan fried in its own juices. Accompanied by fresh vegetable, mixed grains and a mushroom cap. Sauce Bordelaise.

Christiania T-Bone Steak *(Cabernet Sauvignon, Pinot Noir, Bordeaux)*   **$12.00**
The classic of all steak cuts! A full pound and a half of carefully aged corn-fed beef for the guest with that "Mountain Man" appetite! Served with our organic mixed grains and fresh vegetable.

~ Some other good things ~

Baked Idaho Potato
Butter, Sour Cream & Chives
$ 1.00

Pan of Fresh Mushrooms
Sauteed or French Fried
$ 1.50

Whole Artichoke
(In Season)
Butter and Mayonnaise
$ 1.50

North Lake Tahoe
HUGO'S ROTISSERIE
Continental

$$

Hotel restaurants rarely make it into this book, but Hugo's at the Hyatt Lake Tahoe is a notable exception. Actually, Hugo's is not in the Hyatt, but located in its own rustic contemporary building right on the shore of the lake. The dining room looks like a gigantic tepee, with the beamed roof pitching upwards to a skylight, through which extends the towering chimney from a central fireplace. The decor is warm and cheerful with chairs and booths upholstered in a handsome print fabric; tables are set with pewter serving plates and ceramic tableware. Hugo's has a simple menu formula that works. First there is a visit to the "greenery bar" which bears little resemblance to the ubiquitous salad bar. There are appetizers like chopped chicken livers, herring in sour cream and, for salads, crisped spinach greens, marinated mushrooms and a savory green-olive relish. Many of the entrées are exquisitely seasoned meat and fowl dishes which are spit-roasted on the open rotisseries at the back of the dining room. These include roast young duckling with a choice of sauces (lingonberry, honey almond, orange or cherry); an outstanding herb-crusted rack of spring lamb Dijon; chicken Sicilian; and grilled petrale sole, all accompanied by fresh vegetables. Dinner at Hugo's ends with a visit to a dessert bar and a complimentary brandy or cognac. Complete dinners are $6.95 to $12.95.

HUGO'S ROTISSERIE, Hyatt Lake Tahoe, Incline Village, Nevada. Telephone: (916) 831-1111. Hours: 6-midnight, nightly. Cards: AE, BA, CB, DC, MC. Reservations advised. Full bar service.

North Lake Tahoe
LAKE HOUSE OF TAHOE
Pizza

$

Many think they have found the perfect pizza here, though "thick-crust" purists may not agree. Lake House's pizza is made with a thin, light crust of whole wheat dough, heaped about two inches high with the freshest ingredients imaginable. There are 22 varieties, plus almost unlimited combinations thereof—Louisiana shrimp, Portuguese linguica sausage, zucchini and tomato, plus all the traditional toppings such as mushrooms, olives, pepperoni, etc., etc. Service is casual on bare-topped tables and the blaring rock and country music can be disconcerting. It does offer an outdoor dining deck, magnificent view of the lake and some of the world's greatest pizza.

LAKE HOUSE OF TAHOE, 600 North Lake Boulevard, Tahoe City. Telephone: (916) 583-2222. Hours: 11-midnight, weekdays; until 1 am on weekends. Cards: BA, MC. Full bar service.

Truckee
LA VIEILLE MAISON
French

$$$

In an historic house near the Truckee River, Robert Charles, one of California's most colorful and venerable restaurateurs, has established a unique restaurant—one that specializes in garlic! He believes that garlic helps the blood circulation, prevents catching colds (no one comes near a garlic eater) and is the "best aphrodisiac in the world." M. Charles, who has owned some of the most noted restaurants in the San Francisco Bay Area (most recently Maurice et Charles Bistrot in Marin), also offers some uncommon dishes as vehicles for garlic. There are brains with wild sage plucked before dawn that morning, codfish in a sauce of fresh tomatoes and onions, and fresh mussels. For an appetizer, try the torte of sliced onions baked in a garlicky cream sauce. The salad, served after the meal, is garnished with pine nuts, raisins and slivers of Gruyère. The old house has had a checkered past. It once served as a rooming house for ice cutters in the days when Truckee supplied ice to cities as far away as New Orleans; in the twenties it was the residence for the film crew of Charlie Chaplin's "Gold Rush"; and at some unspecified time it was reportedly a bordello. The building has been elegantly restored in turn-of-the-century decor.

LA VIEILLE MAISON, Highway 267, Truckee. Telephone: (916) 587-2421. Dinner: Wednesday-Sunday. Brunch: 11:30-2:30, Saturday and Sunday. Cards: BA, MC. Full bar service.

SON MENU

All our dishes are served a la carte, seasoned with fresh garlic

TERRINE DU CHASSEUR   2.50
   (the Chef's pate)

TOURTE AUX OIGNONS ET AULX   2.00
   (Onions and garlic, cream, pastry crust)

CHAMPIGNONS GLAÇES DU LEVANT   2.25
   (Mushrooms cold, with herbs)

CONSOMME A L'AIL   1.75
   (Garlic consomme)

CRÊME DE LÉGUMES   1.75
   (Creamed fresh vegetable soup)

MOULES MARINIÈRE   7.50
   (Fresh mussels Fisherman's style)

TOURNEDOS BRAVADE   8.50
   (Beef filet provencal sauce)

LEGUMES MÉDITERRANEÉN   5.50
   (Vegetarian fresh vegetable plate)

LE PLAT DU JOUR
   (Chef's daily specialty)

CERVELLES À LA SAUGE SAUVAGE
DE TRUCKEE   6.50
   (Brains, wild sage)

MORUE SAUCE BOURRIDE   7.50
   (Codfish, spiced tomato sauce)

SALADE FRISEE AUX CHAPONS   2.00
   (Chicoree salad, garlic croutons)

SALADE FANTAISIE   2.00
   (Lettuce, pignolias, raisins, gruyere)

For those who think they are allergic:
POINTE DE BOEUF À L'ÉCHALOTE   9.00
   (Steak with shallots)

Truckee
O'B'S BOARD
American (Western) $$

Main Street, Truckee, probably hasn't changed that much
from its railroading days and O'B's Board looks very much
like a turn-of-the-century restaurant. Lace curtains, antique
sideboards, brass chandeliers and Victorian settees turn the
bar into an old-fashioned living room. Flocked wallpaper
covers the dining room walls and an antique kitchen stove
has been commandeered for a salad bar. Here your waiter
mixes up a bountiful garden salad of romaine, garbanzos,
red cabbage, carrots, zucchini and cherry tomatoes. This is
included in the dinner price ($5.50 to $7.95), along with
freshly baked sourdough bread. The entrées of steaks,
shrimp, turkey, beef kabob or barbecued ribs are simply
prepared but hearty. For dessert try the homemade banana-
nut bread topped with vanilla ice cream and blueberries.

O'B'S BOARD, Main Street, Truckee. Telephone: (916)
587-4164. Hours: 5:30-10:30, daily; closed Thanksgiving
and Christmas. Cards: BA, MC. Reservations not accepted.
Full bar service. Street parking.

North Lake Tahoe
PETIT PIER
French $$

From France chef Jean Dufau came to California by way of
Caesar's Palace in Las Vegas. Some years back he spruced
up two motel rooms in Tahoe Vista with fishnets and
nautical memorabilia and opened a tiny bistro, where diners
suffered incredibly crammed quarters to enjoy his fine
French cooking. Several years ago Petit Pier moved into a

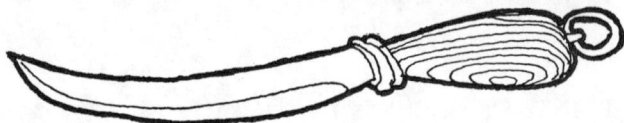

slightly larger, but vastly more elegant place next door, with red and white wallpaper and a view of the lake. Today it is generally acclaimed as Tahoe's finest restaurant, though some detractors object to the still crowded and often noisy conditions. But the food cannot be equaled at the lake. Dufau makes a great effort to bring in fresh seafood from the East Coast and, season permitting, you might find soft shell crabs, mussels or sweet scallops on that night's menu. Of the meat dishes, a filet of lamb for two in a puff pastry shell is a house specialty, as are the duckling Montmorency and steak au poivre, both flamed at the table. You might start your dinner here with a romaine and Roquefort salad, smoked salmon, or melon and prosciutto, freshly sliced from hams hung to dry in the dining room. Prices are all à la carte here with entrées in the $7 to $11 range. You can easily spend $15 per person for food alone.

PETIT PIER, 7252 North Lake Boulevard, Tahoe Vista. Telephone: (916) 546-4464. Hours: 6-9:30, daily; closed Tuesdays in the winter. Cards: AE, BA, MC. Reservations advised. Wine only.

North Lake Tahoe
SQUIRREL'S NEST
Soup and Sandwiches $

Nestled among the tall Tahoe pines, in back of a charming little shop, is one of the most popular spots at the lake for al fresco lunches. If the imaginative soups and sandwiches, the gorgeous salads seem familiar, you have probably had them at Sausalito's Soupçon, whose proprietors run the Squirrel's Nest kitchen in the summer months. If you order ahead of time, they'll prepare a packed lunch for a lakeside picnic.

SQUIRREL'S NEST, 5405 West Lake Boulevard, Homewood. Telephone: (916) 525-7944. Hours: noon-3:30, daily, June through Labor Day. No cards. Reservations not necessary. Wine only. Parking lot.

Index

GEOGRAPHICAL

INDEX BY CUISINE

Area Abbreviations:
SF: San Francisco
Mar: Marin County
EB: East Bay
Pen: Peninsula
MA: Monterey Area
NSM: Napa/Sonoma/
            Mendocino
CV: Central Valley
ML: Mother Lode
LT: Lake Tahoe Area

Chinese

China Camp (CV), 173
Far East Cafe (SF), 38
Five Happiness (SF), 39
Hunan (SF), 47
Imperial Dynasty (CV), 182
The Mandarin (SF), 68
Pierre's Wah Yen (Pen), 138
Szechwan (SF), 88
Taiwan Restaurant (EB),
  125
Tao Tao Cafe (Pen), 139
Tung Fong (SF), 96
Yank Sing (SF), 98

Continental

Argonaut Inn (ML), 185
Blue Fox (SF), 18
Butterworth's (ML), 186
Cafe Mozart (SF), 21
Christiania Inn (LT), 192
Club XIX (MA), 141
Depot Hotel (NSM), 161
Golden Eagle (SF), 44
Grey Fox Inn (MA), 158
The Hamlet (MA), 159
Hugo's Rotisserie (LT), 194
La Bohême (MA), 147
Ledford House (NSM), 164
Liaison (Pen), 135
Narsai's (EB), 120
Oliver's (NSM), 168
Pine Brook Inn (Pen), 136
Soupçon (Mar), 110-111
The Ram (CV), 177
Whaling Station Inn (MA),
  157

Czech

Manka's (Mar), 106

English

Butterworth's (ML), 186

French

À La Carte (EB), 114
Alexis (SF), 14
Au Relais (NSM), 162
Chez Felix (MA), 142
Chez Joseph (EB), 115
Chez Leon (SF), 26
Chez Michel (SF), 28
Chez Villaret (LT), 191
City Hotel (ML), 187
Emile's Swiss Affair
  (Pen), 128
Fleur de Lys (SF), 40
Guernica (Mar), 101
Imperial Dynasty (CV), 182
La Bonne Auberge (Pen),
  134
La Maisonette (SF), 54
La Marmite (Mar), 102
La Mirabelle (SF), 52
La Terrasse (Pen), 130
La Vieille Maison (LT), 196
Le Club (SF), 60
Le Coq d'Or (MA), 148-149
Le Cyrano (SF), 62
L'Étoile (SF), 64
Le Pot au Feu (Pen), 132-133
Little River Cafe (NSM), 166
L'Orangerie (SF), 66
Maison Bergerac (MA), 150
Maurice et Charles Bistrot
  (Mar), 108
Oscar's Bistro (EB), 122
Pâtisserie Boissière (MA),
  149
Petit Pier (LT), 198-199
Restaurant La Salle (CV),
  178
Rue de Polk (SF), 80
Wulff's (CV), 180

Philippine
Love's Pagan's Den (EB),
119

Pizza
Lake House of Tahoe (LT),
195

Polish
Warszawa (EB), 126

Russian
Alexis (SF), 14

Seafood
Abalonetti (MA), 146
Flaherty's Oyster Bar (MA),
146-147
Sam's Grill (SF), 84
Seven Seas (Mar), 110
Swan Oyster Depot (SF), 90
Tadich Grill (SF), 91

Soups and Sandwiches
Bon Appétit (NSM), 170
The Brinn House (ML), 185-
186
The Chutney Kitchen
(NSM), 170-171
Napa Valley Cheese Com-
pany (NSM), 170
Squirrel's Nest (LT), 199
Vintage Cafe (NSM), 171

Spanish
El Meson (SF), 34
Pabellón Español (SF), 82

Swiss
Emile's Swiss Affair (Pen),
128
Swiss Cellar (Mar), 111

Thai
Khan Toke (SF), 50

Viennese
Manka's (Mar), 106

Vietnamese
Aux Delices (SF), 20
Saigon Royal (SF), 83

SAN FRANCISCO BAY AREA FOR LATE SUPPERS (Open at least until midnight)

Alexis (SF), 14
Chez Michel (SF), 28
Korea House (SF), 51
Le Club (SF), 60
L'Orangerie (SF), 66
Love's Pagan's Den (EB),
119
The Mandarin (SF), 68
Mario's (SF), 71
North Beach Restaurant
(SF), 74
Pabellón Español (SF), 82
Paprikás Fono (SF), 78
Sapporo-ya (SF), 87
Trader Vic's (SF), 94

SAN FRANCISCO BAY AREA FOR BRUNCH

Cafe Mozart (SF), 21
Caravansary (SF), 24
Lorenzo's (Mar), 104
Mama's (SF), 70
Pine Brook Inn (Pen), 136
Venetian Glass Nephew
(SF), 97

KEEP CURRENT ON CALIFORNIA'S EVER-CHANGING RESTAURANT SCENE By subscribing to California Critic the award-winning monthly newsletter written by the editors of Best Restaurants

NOW IN NORTHERN AND SOUTHERN EDITIONS

You'll be the first to know about exciting new restaurants as we discover them, many in the under $6 price range. You'll save money by hearing about our test visits to famous and expensive restaurants, where the food and service are not worth the price. And you'll receive up-to-date reports on restaurants whose chef or owners have changed. California Critic is published monthly in Northern and Southern editions. Each edition contains reviews of five restaurants in that area, plus a lengthy report on dining out at popular resort areas from Mendocino to Mexico. There is also an article on wine and the popular Bear Flag Reports, humorous and informative news and trivia about the state-wide restaurant scene.

Subscription price is only $20 per year for 12 issues; $35 for two years. Cut out the facing card and send it to California Critic, 834 Mission Street, San Francisco, California 94103. We'll start your subscription immediately and bill you. If you're not pleased with your first issue, just return the bill marked "cancel" and there is no further obligation.

Please enroll me as a subscriber to California Critic and bill me for one year (12 issues) @ $20. I understand that if I am not pleased with the first issue I may return the bill marked "cancel" with no further obligation.

☐ Send Northern California Edition   ☐ Send Southern California Edition

NAME _____

ADDRESS _____

CITY _____ STATE _____ ZIP _____